The Gardener's Guide to Growing Orchids

Charles Marden Fitch

EDITOR

Janet Marinelli
SERIES EDITOR

Sigrun Wolff Saphire
SENIOR EDITOR

David Horak
TECHNICAL EDITOR

Kerry Barringer
SCIENCE EDITOR

Leah Kalotay
ART DIRECTOR

Joni Blackburn
COPY EDITOR

Steven Clemants
VICE-PRESIDENT,
SCIENCE &
PUBLICATIONS

Judith D. Zuk
PRESIDENT

Elizabeth Scholtz
DIRECTOR
EMERITUS

All photographs by
Charles Marden Fitch,
except as noted on
page 114.

Handbook #178

Copyright © 2004 by Brooklyn Botanic Garden, Inc.

All-Region Guides, formerly *21st-Century Gardening Series,* are published three times a year at 1000 Washington Ave., Brooklyn, NY 11225.

Subscription included in Brooklyn Botanic Garden subscriber membership dues ($35 per year; $45 outside the United States).

ISBN # 1-889538-61-2

Printed by Science Press, a division of the Mack Printing Group. Printed on recycled paper.

Above: *Epidendrum* **'Talisman Cove' (***E.* **Star Valley** × *E.* **Shizuno Muraoka).**
Cover: *Cymbidium* **Goldrun 'Cooksbridge' AM/AOS.**

The Gardener's Guide to Growing Orchids

Cultivating Orchids

David Horak

The cultivation of orchids has a long history marked by triumphant successes and spectacular failures. For more than 200 years, people have endeavored to grow these wonderful plants, little by little expanding our collective body of horticultural knowledge. In 1789, 15 different tropical orchid species were in cultivation at what would become the Royal Botanic Gardens, Kew, England. Within the next 50 years, orchid mania had swept Europe, and the tropical forests around the globe were yielding up hundreds of new species to the countless explorers sent out by wealthy collectors.

In the early years, orchid growing was a complicated and expensive proposition. Avid growers assumed that orchids came from hot steamy jungles much like the dense coastal forests surrounding the equatorial seaports from which many of the plants were shipped. They mimicked this steamy environment in their greenhouses, keeping their precious plants in deep shade and constant, unventilated heat, combined with extreme humidity and plenty of water. The oppressive conditions in the hothouses, cynically referred to as stoves, killed many of the few orchids that had survived the long months of shipping at sea. A few plants managed to live long enough to bloom, however, fueling the desire for more orchids. But as every seasoned orchid grower has come to learn from painful experience, orchids not only send out a flower spike and bloom as a reward for good culture but also as a last-gasp attempt to reproduce before dying.

Cultivating tropical orchids used to be a complicated and expensive proposition, but these days orchids such as this *Cymbidium* Mary Pinchess CCM/AOS have become popular houseplants.

Most orchids in cultivation are epiphytic plants from tropical climates, such as this *Pholidota* species growing at about 4,500 feet in Thailand. In the home or greenhouse, orchids do best when growing conditions resemble those of their native habitat, or in the case of hybrids, the habitat of their ancestors.

Over time, gardeners found out that most tropical orchids come from breezy, humid, moderate climates and need bright light and plenty of fresh air to grow. They removed the heavy shading from the greenhouses and opened the vents to let in fresh air and light and to moderate temperatures. Finally the orchids began to thrive.

Most orchids in cultivation today are epiphytic plants from tropical climates. In nature, they grow on trees and other plants, and their thick, fleshy roots clasp the tree bark in search of moisture and nutrients. Though it's true that most thrive in regions with abundant rainfall, the plants always require excellent drainage and plenty of fresh air. The challenge for the orchid gardener is to identify the specific needs of every plant and find the right balance of elements that make a plant thrive: proper temperatures; adequate amounts of water, light, fertilizer, humidity, and air movement; and an amenable growing medium.

Orchidists are constantly looking to improve their collections, frequently experimenting with new growing media, cultural techniques, fertilizers, and regimens. Many books have been written about raising orchids, but much information continues to be passed anecdotally from grower to grower—hard won by decades of trial and error. Unfortunately, along with the valuable and accurate information comes plenty of dubious suppositions and unsubstantiated claims. Since there are few hard and fast rules, novices will invariably come across confusing or contradictory instructions.

Always try to remain flexible, and be prepared to do a little research when in doubt. Find out as much as possible about the native habitats of the plants you want to grow, or about their ancestors if you are growing hybrids. New books on general orchid culture appear regularly, but beyond the beginner level, the most useful books are specialized works comprehensively discussing the needs of specific genera or groups. Scientific monographs, floras, and encyclopedias that describe orchid species, their native habitats, and how they grow are also useful. Several exceptional online encyclopedias and Web pages dedicated to specific genera and alliances make it easier than ever to locate information. For tips on books and other useful sources, see "For More Information," page 109.

As convenient and reassuring as it is to sit down at a computer and have a world of information at your fingertips, remember that nothing can replace seeing live plants in bloom and talking to other orchid growers. Visit or join orchid societies in your area to meet other orchid enthusiasts and talk with knowledgeable people. Research, read, and compare notes with other orchid enthusiasts, but bear this in mind: If a particular technique works for you, don't make changes just because a book or another person says what you are doing is wrong. As a good friend and experienced grower frequently reminds me, "Orchids don't read books."

Buying Orchids

Plants and supplies are readily available from many different sources. Orchid societies are often a great place to acquire plants. Most have raffles of plants or annual orchid auctions, and often vendors or members sell plants at a society's monthly meetings. Trading with

Decent orchids may be available at your local supermarket. However, for practical advice along with good-quality plants, head to orchid society events or specialty nurseries.

other growers can be a great way to obtain rare and unusual plants. At times even supermarkets and discount centers can be good sources for decent plants at good prices, but of course, they are not the best places to get advice on how to grow orchids. Commercial firms that specialize in raising orchids offer a much greater selection and better quality. Visit an orchid nursery in person if it accommodates visitors, but you can also easily and safely purchase orchids from catalogs, online, or at orchid shows. If you don't see what you are looking for in a catalog, ask for it: Most dealers don't list plants if they have only small quantities available.

Keep in mind that dealers usually avoid shipping plants in winter to areas that commonly experience below-freezing temperatures. Even with the best packing and express delivery, leaves or inflorescences can get damaged in transit at any time of the year. If the packaging seems reasonable, try to overlook minor damage. If a plant arrives with a broken leaf or pseudobulb, remove the damaged plant part with a sterile razor blade and dust the cut end with cinnamon or Neosporin ointment to minimize the chances of infection. In the event of significant damage, immediately contact both the vendor and the carrier to determine the best course of action. If the quality or condition of the plants differs significantly from the catalog description or if the plants are dead, call the vendor immediately. Reputable firms stand behind their plants and will provide reasonable recourse.

Grow the best plants that you can find and afford. It takes just as much work to grow a plant of inferior quality as it takes to grow a good one. Beauty may be in the eye of the beholder, but the qualities that orchid judges look for in all flowers, those that set them apart from the merely average, are generally consistent. In general, look for flowers that are large for their type, with full, wide segments. Color and markings should be clear, and the flowers should be

Online and mail-order catalogs offer a wide selection of plants, but bear in mind that most dealers avoid shipping plants in winter to areas that commonly experience temperatures below freezing.

Vanda sanderiana Alba 'Eastwind' HCC/AOS. The letters behind the name show that the flower has won one of the much-sought-after American Orchid Society awards, an indication of quality that may be helpful when choosing a plant.

well presented on their inflorescences without excessive crowding, or the need for excessive staking. See also "How Orchids are Judged," page 107.

One clue to identifying a quality plant is to look for a clonal or cultivar name after the genus and species or hybrid name. This name appears in single quotes, as in *Lycaste* Jackpot 'Willow Pond'. An even better indication is an American Orchid Society or Royal Horticultural Society award abbreviation appended to its name, for example: *Slc.* Tiny Titan 'Laval' HCC/AOS or *Cattleya* Portia 'Cannizaro' AM/RHS. Sometimes the parentage of an orchid is listed as an indication of its potential quality, for example *Phragmipedium* Twilight 4N (Eric Young 4N 'Haley Suzanne' AM/AOS × Living Fire 4N 'Prometheus' FCC/AOS). Both parents have high American Orchid Society awards, and "4N" after each name indicates that each plant is a tetraploid version and likely to have larger flowers with heavier substance. For more information on orchid awards, see "Showing Orchids," page 102.

Avoid expensive rare species and hybrids for your first orchids, no matter how gorgeous they look, especially if you don't have a greenhouse. Conversely, try not to buy an unlabeled plant or one that comes with just a partial name such as *Phalaenopsis* hybrid. The plant may be pretty, but you may eventually want to show it in an exhibit or on a show table, or present it for judging, and in all these instances a complete name is required.

Look for plants with clean, healthy, turgid leaves and pseudobulbs. Preferably you should be able to see live roots extending into the medium, which itself should not be too decomposed. It is common for epiphytic orchids to have roots growing out of the pots into the air. Do not be concerned. The exposed roots should have live green or reddish tips. Avoid plants that look desiccated or have an abundance of black spots on the leaves, dead leaf tips, bugs, or weeds growing in the pots.

Most growers, especially beginners, are best served with mature blooming-size plants. Look to see if the plant has previously bloomed so you know that you're getting a mature plant likely to bloom when its flowering season comes. Buying seedlings may be tempting since the cute little plants are cheaper, but it typically takes from three to five years before they reach flowering size, and younger plants often demand more care than mature ones. Seedlings can provide great opportunities for experienced growers who have the space and the patience to nurse them to mature size.

In the beginning it's also better to avoid acquiring orchids attached to mounts such as branches or tree fern plaques. The naturalistic presentation may be very appealing, and most orchids can grow well cultivated in this way, but they usually need higher humidity and typically require daily watering.

Growing Requirements

Light

Light is undoubtedly the most important factor in determining whether or not an orchid will flower. Not only is the intensity of available light important, but its quality and duration need to be considered as well. Lower light levels available for longer periods of time can be nearly as effective as brighter light for a shorter time. There are limits, of course, but this principle is the basis for the successful culture of orchids under artificial light. Growing orchids under lights is more challenging but more controllable once the basics are understood. For more information on this topic, see "Growing Orchids Under Lights," page 40.

How much light do orchids need? The rule of thumb is to provide as much light as the orchid's leaves can take without burning. Put simply, orchids should have bright light green leaves, and the growths should be strong and compact. With too little light the leaves are elongated and narrow, and the stems and pseudobulbs do not support themselves well. Plants with luxurious dark green leaves due to low light conditions may look healthy and beautiful but may rarely, if ever, bloom.

There are tremendous variations in the amount of light different orchids need to bloom. *Phalaenopsis* are among the least demanding, requiring relative low light levels to succeed. Paphiopedilums need slightly brighter light. Orchids in the *Cattleya*, *Dendrobium*, and *Oncidium* alliances require fairly bright, lightly shaded conditions. A good way to test whether there is enough light on your windowsill or under your plant lights for an orchid to bloom is to hold your hand approximately one foot over the top of the plant at the brightest

In the home, place orchids such as this mini *Cymbidium* close to the window and use curtains or light shading to regulate the amount of sunlight they receive.

time of day, to see how strong a shadow is cast. A very slight shadow indicates that there is sufficient light for a *Phalaenopsis* to bloom. A strong clearly defined shadow means there should be enough light for a *Cattleya* to bloom.

Vandas and their relatives need the brightest conditions possible short of full sun. Occasionally, growers succeed in bringing a vandaceous orchid to bloom on a windowsill or under artificial lights (to the accolades and admiration of their peers), but in general these orchids tend to be better suited to growing in a greenhouse, or at least summering outdoors.

Light intensity is usually measured in foot-candles. Full midday summer sun, for example, can reach intensities as high as 10,000 foot-candles. The majority of orchids require roughly between 1,000 and 4,000 foot-candles of light for at least four hours a day in order to grow well and bloom. In a greenhouse, this level of light is relatively easy to attain. In fact, most greenhouses need approximately 50 percent shading if the orchids are to do well. This is usually achieved either with a specialized open-weave shade cloth stretched over the greenhouse for most of the year or a light coating of whitewash on the exterior of the glass. In the home or apartment, 1,000 foot-candles approximates the brightest light available within one foot of an unobstructed window with an eastern exposure; it is often referred to as bright shade. The light available in a window with an unshaded south or west exposure, where a distinct, clearly defined shadow can be cast, as described above, is approximately 3,000 to 4,000 foot-candles. Farther away from a window the light intensity falls off dramatically. While there are exceptions and mitigating circumstances, an orchid that's more than two feet away from the average window may grow well but will probably not flower. In the home it is best to place orchids as close to the windows as possible and use curtains or light shading to control the amount of sun coming in. An eastern exposure is probably the most accommodating, as it is bright enough to bring many plants to flower but unlikely to cause plants to get sunburned. A lightly shaded southern exposure offers a longer day length and may make it possible to grow the greatest variety of orchids with differing needs. No matter where you grow your orchids, remember that the aspect of the sun changes from low on the horizon in winter, with short days, to high in the sky in summer, with long days. This change can result in quite dramatic seasonal differences

in the amount of light the plants receive and may necessitate moving them. Be especially vigilant in early spring and early fall—the stronger light may burn delicate foliage in less than an hour.

If you have a porch or backyard, you can move your orchids outside during the warmer seasons. The balmy temperatures, constant air movement, and natural light are beneficial for the plants, which may profit tremendously from a summer spent outdoors. However, proceed

Cattleya Irene Holguin with a sunburned leaf. If they get too much sun, delicate orchid leaves can burn in an hour or less, especially in early spring and fall, when the sun is low on the horizon.

Orchids and other tropical plants benefit from spending the summer outdoors. Natural light, fresh air, and air movement are all beneficial for the plants. Be careful to expose plants slowly to the brighter light conditions outside to avoid sunburn. And be sure to move them back inside before it gets too cold in fall.

with care: Leaves can burn very easily outdoors. As little as ten minutes of direct sun can cause severe lesions that appear as pale yellow to white patches. The damage may impair the look of the plant for several years; if the burns are severe, they may lead to the plant's demise. Orchids usually do fine in unshaded morning and late-afternoon sun but must be protected from full midday sun. Set them under a tree or shrub, by a fence, or anywhere there is some dappled shade. When first moving a plant outside for the season, let it slowly get used to the brighter light by increasing the level of exposure over several days.

In a bright unshaded window or greenhouse, orchid leaves may also burn because the glass can magnify the effects of the sun's rays. This most often happens in the spring when the days become longer and the sun climbs higher in the sky. Feel the temperature of the leaves. If the leaves feel hot, move the plant to a shadier location or provide supplemental shading.

Some orchids are photoperiod sensitive, which means they bloom seasonally in response to a short or long day length. Regardless of where you grow orchids, avoid

Dendrobium Palolo Sunshine 'Bronze Warrior' HCC/AOS needs fairly bright light to bloom. If the light in your growing area isn't right for the plant, it may still be lush and green but will probably bloom sparingly and irregularly or not at all.

having other lights go on and off at irregular intervals or exposing the plants to a 24-hour light source. In the home or office and in many urban areas, this may be nearly impossible, and as result, some plants may bloom irregularly or not at all.

Watering

Watering frequency depends on the growing medium, time of year, state of plant activity, and environmental conditions, and it should not be done on a fixed schedule. Different growing media vary in their degree of water retention, but a good rule of thumb is to water the medium as it approaches dryness. Generally, watering needs to be more frequent, perhaps two or three times a week, during the growing season when the plants are active and the days are long. In the fall and winter when growths have matured and the days get shorter, the plants may only need to be watered once every seven to ten days. Sometimes a light sprinkling may be all that is required.

If you are not sure whether an orchid needs to be watered, lift the pot and judge its weight; a dry pot weighs less than a wet one. When in doubt, wait another day or two before you water. Always keep in mind that more orchids are killed by overwatering than underwatering.

When it's time to water, do so thoroughly, making sure to use cool to tepid water. Both hot and cold water can seriously damage roots and leaves. Water until the medium is completely wet and water runs out of the bottom of the pot. Water from the top rather than the bottom, since most potting media float. Never dunk several plants in a shared bucket in an attempt to save water or fertilizer. It's an ideal way to spread disease from plant to plant, especially viruses. Occasionally wet or wash all plant parts to remove dust and sticky plant secretions. This will help reduce the chances of insect problems. But don't allow water to get on the leaves when the plants are in very bright light or direct sun—the water droplets can magnify the light intensity, and the leaves can get burned.

Ideally, water early in the day so that the leaves are dry by nightfall. Water left on the leaves and in the leaf axils (where the leaf meets the stem) promotes infection with bacterial or fungal diseases that can disfigure or kill a plant or cause an emerging inflorescence or new growth to rot.

Watering needs also change with the weather. Try not to water on cloudy, cool, wet, or humid days. Minimize watering during periods of prolonged cloudy and rainy weather; increase the humidity in the growing area instead. When it's sunny, hot, and dry, you will most certainly have to water your orchids more. However, watering during hot, humid weather, especially when the nights are hot, can promote root rot in orchids that prefer cooler conditions. Water lightly and rely on light sprinklings rather than heavy watering.

Most orchids can survive, not thrive, if kept too dry, but overwatering can kill an orchid within a couple of days. The leaves and pseudobulbs become lax and start to shrivel because

Lack of water and low humidity has caused the leaves of this *Miltonia* to emerge wrinkled. To avoid such problems, adjust watering and growing conditions according to the plant's needs.

Growing *Ascocenda* Sandy Schultz in a basket allows for good air circulation around the epiphytic plant's root system and assures excellent drainage.

the root system is rotting and the plant can no longer take in moisture. At this time an inexperienced grower might assume that the plant is not getting enough water and respond accordingly, thus compounding the problem. The right response is to remove the plant from its pot and inspect the roots. If they are soggy, brown, and dead, trim them back to live tissue and repot the plant in new medium and let it dry. Keep the humidity high and light levels low and hope for new root growth. If you don't intervene in time, opportunistic bacterial rots will soon turn the plant to mush.

If the roots appear whitish but shriveled and the medium is dry, the plant has received too little water. Replace it in its pot and move it to a humid location. Water lightly and gradually increase the frequency of watering until the stems, leaves, and roots begin to plump.

Water quality is very important for plant health. Clean rainwater is ideal for orchids. It normally has a slightly acidic to neutral pH of about 6.9 to 7.0, with virtually no dissolved minerals. Water from most municipal water systems and well water are generally adequate but vary considerably in quality. Water with a very low pH (acidic) or a very high pH (alkaline or basic) that contains high levels of dissolved minerals such as calcium and magnesium can damage plants and impede nutrient uptake, literally starving plants. While both calcium and magnesium are important plant nutrients, they can occur in forms that are not usable to plants. In many places, especially those relying on well water, the water is hard, with over 200 ppm of dissolved solids and a high or low pH. (A reading over 120 ppm is considered hard water, whereas soft water will have 60 ppm or under.) Very hard water leaves a whitish film or powder on the leaves and growing medium when the water evaporates. The film is usually considered unsightly but only a cosmetic issue. However, if enough minerals accumulate, they can block light absorption and impede photosynthesis.

Orchids can tolerate a pH from about 5.0 to about 8.5. Municipal systems are regularly monitored and treated, so you can request an analysis from your local water department to find out how your tap water rates. Most cities add chlorine to the water to kill pathogens. Chlorine is usually not a significant problem, but it may cause some root damage or leaf-tip dieback in more sensitive plants. If it proves to be a problem, try running the water through an activated charcoal filter system or let the water stand in a bucket for 24 hours to allow the chlorine to evaporate.

You can also use a filtration system such as reverse osmosis (RO). The result is excellent water with virtually no dissolved solids. In fact, it's important to add some fertilizer or unfiltered tap water to both RO and distilled water to prevent the water from robbing nutrients from the plants through osmosis.

Temperatures

Different authorities may disagree on the ideal temperature ranges for certain orchids, but most people put orchids into one of three categories: warm-growing (90°F maximum temperature on a summer day to 65°F minimum temperature on a winter night), intermediate (85°F to 60°F), or cool-growing (75°F to 55°F). Most tropical orchids are content with daytime highs from 75°F to 80°F and nighttime temperatures that are about 10 to 15 degrees cooler. The diurnal drop in temperature is very important for the plants to produce strong growths and, in many cases, to initiate blooming. Orchids grown in buildings with climate-control systems that maintain stable, nearly

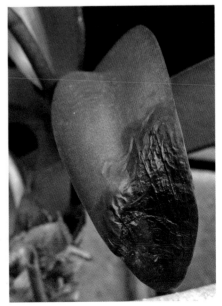

This orchid leaf has suffered frost damage from sitting too near a cold window during freezing weather.

The Right Plant for the Right Spot

You don't need a greenhouse to grow a variety of orchids indoors. Take advantage of the different microclimates in your home to accommodate plants with varying needs. Different parts of the house may be warmer or cooler, lighter or shadier. Because there are orchids for almost any kind of environment, it is possible to grow different kinds of orchids even without an expensive glasshouse or artificial-light setup.

North-, south-, east-, and west-facing windows obviously have different degrees of exposure to sunlight. And on every windowsill light exposure varies from one side to the other and throughout the seasons. For example, in the winter, the right side of a window with western exposure is sunnier than the left side (in the Northern Hemisphere). The right side of a west-facing windowsill is a good wintertime environment for dendrobiums or cattleyas, whereas paphiopedilums and *Phalaenopsis* are better suited to the lower light levels on the left side of the sill. In the summertime when the sun is higher and stronger, the left side of a west-facing windowsill may be too sunny for the paphs and phals, and they may have to be moved to another location. By the same token, one part of a windowsill may be drier than the other if it is closer to a radiator or air conditioner.

Become aware of the many microclimates in your home and choose orchids

best suited to the various conditions. And keep in mind that if a plant isn't doing well in one spot, this doesn't necessarily mean that you can't grow it. Try moving it to another microclimate that better meets its needs.

By taking advantage of the microclimates on your windowsill, you can find perfect spots to grow a variety of beautiful orchids in a relatively small area in your home. Be sure to watch carefully as the seasons change to avoid problems caused by too much or too little light.

constant temperatures may not experience sufficient variation in temperature to bloom. For most plants, temperatures over 90°F are damaging. When the daytime highs exceed the recommendations for a plant, try improving conditions by increasing humidity and air movement and by providing additional shading.

Orchids such as *Phalaenopsis* and *Cattleya* types will be harmed if temperatures drop below 50°F. If you are moving your orchids outdoors for the summer, wait until nighttime temperatures are regularly 55°F and above. In fall, move the plants back inside before the nights become too cold. But always be sure to check the needs of individual orchids. Cymbidiums, for example, require nighttime temperatures in the low 40s in the fall to initiate flower spikes.

If you are growing orchids on a windowsill, be particularly careful in winter when the temperature close by the window can easily fall below freezing and potentially damage leaves or even kill plants.

Humidity Levels

Humidity is most often measured as a percentage of the amount of moisture actually in the air relative to the air's capacity to hold it. As air heats up, its ability to hold moisture increases substantially. Most orchids tolerate humidity ranges from about 40 to 80 percent. Within this range, higher humidity levels accommodate more types of orchids and produce better growth and fewer problems with blooming. Humidity is often highest early in the morning when temperatures are cooler, then it steadily declines as the temperatures rise. The amount of moisture in the air has stayed the same, but the capacity of the air to hold moisture has increased, so the relative humidity drops. In order to maintain higher humidity levels, more moisture is needed.

Too little humidity often causes buds or inflorescences to become stuck in their sheaths, and as the flowers try to emerge they get twisted and deformed. In the worst cases they will desiccate and die. Low humidity can also keep new leads (vegetative growths) from emerging properly and result in wrinkled, accordion-pleat leaves. This is a common problem with *Oncidium*-type plants, especially *Miltoniopsis*. The leaves may be unsightly but the condition is rarely damaging to a plant unless it is severe enough to cause the loss of a leaf. Raising the humidity will take care of all of these problems.

It is fairly easy to achieve adequate humidity in a greenhouse with the help of humidifying foggers, misters, or by wetting down the floors on a regular basis. In the home or office it can be difficult to maintain adequate levels of humidity. In summer, air-conditioning draws moisture out of the air, and during the winter the ambient relative humidity can easily drop below 10 percent in a centrally heated room. A humidifier placed close to the plants can usually provide enough humidity. Even misting the plants occasionally during the day with a spray bottle can help. When the humidity is adequate, the rate at which a plant gives off moisture through its leaves is balanced. It is important to remember that it's not possible to compensate for low humidity by increasing watering. When the humidity is low, a plant will often transpire faster than the water can move through its system to compensate. It becomes desiccated yet may lose its roots because of excessive moisture in its pot.

Many people set their plants on shallow trays lined with gravel and partially filled with water, so that the pots are just above water level. The premise is that the evaporation of the water will raise the humidity around the plants. In practice, without enclosing plants and trays to confine the evaporated moisture, water will quickly dissipate into the environment without effectively raising the humidity level. The best reason for setting the plants on trays is to make watering easier, as the trays catch the excess runoff when the orchids are watered in place. In this way orchid growers might be more inclined to water whenever the plants need it rather than try to postpone the job of hauling the plants to the sink or shower for as long as possible.

In the evening, as temperatures sink and the ability of the air to hold moisture decreases, the humidity begins to rise. In response, it's best to turn off humidifiers to prevent moisture from condensing on the plants. In general, when the humidity is too high and there is little air circulation, conditions are just right for the spread of fungal and bacterial disease problems. Of course, in nature plants are commonly wet at night, but they are exposed to constant air movement, which prevents the stagnant conditions that can lead to problems.

Fresh Air and Air Movement

Fresh air and air circulation are vital for orchids grown in the home or greenhouse. The plants' leaves should move gently in a light breeze created by constantly running fans. Oscillating fans are the best choice; they are better at providing active air movement than fixed straight-line fans. Good air movement delivers oxygen and carbon dioxide to the leaves, helps keep leaf temperatures down when it is hot and sunny, and allows foliage to dry quickly after watering, minimizing disease problems. Air movement is a key component to be considered when trying to balance watering,

A plastic pot is a suitable home for *Masdevallia strobelii* 'Janet', which needs to stay constantly damp. As with all other orchids, it also needs good air movement to assure that its foliage dries quickly after watering.

Growing orchids in a greenhouse offers many advantages, such as higher humidity levels than easily accomplished in the home, more variation in microclimates, and more light levels.

humidity, light, and temperatures in a healthy environment. While good air circulation is important, the growing area should not be a wind tunnel. Too much air movement, especially if combined with low humidity, can pull moisture from the plants and desiccate them.

Fertilizing Orchids

It used to be assumed that as epiphytes, or air plants, orchids did not need fertilizing because in nature the plants are commonly attached to tree limbs with little or no humus or other obvious organic source of nutrition available. While we now know this is not the case, the nutritional needs of many orchids are still a mystery to orchid growers.

Much of what plants need in order to thrive is readily available in the growing medium or the environment, but there are 13 mineral nutrients that become depleted and must be replenished on a regular basis. The three primary macronutrients, nitrogen (N), phosphorus (P), and potassium (K), often shortened to NPK, are usually indicated in a fertilizer as a numerical ratio such as 30-10-10, 20-20-20, or the like. The three numbers indicate the percentage of each nutrient in the formula. In addition, plants need smaller quantities of other minerals, such as the secondary macronutrients calcium (Ca), magnesium (Mg), and sulfur (S), and seven micronutrients, or what are frequently termed trace elements, boron (B), copper (Cu), iron (Fe), chloride (Cl), manganese (Mn), molybdenum (Mo), and zinc (Zn).

Specific fertilizer compositions and regimens vary tremendously from grower to grower. Inorganic fertilizers that use combinations of mineral salts, soluble in water, are the easiest to use and most commonly available. Manufacturers offer a variety of different formulations specific to the needs of different plants in either liquid or powder form.

In the early days of orchid cultivation, osmunda fiber was the medium of choice; it required almost no additional nutrients to succeed with orchids. But for the past 40 years or so, as fir bark has become the most common growing medium, regular supplemental fertilizing has been necessary since the bark provides little in the way of nutrition for the plants as it breaks down. Some growers fertilize at full strength every fourth watering when the plants are actively growing. I support the time-worn adage of feeding "weakly weekly." Orchids are generally considered to be light feeders. So, when orchids are actively growing, commercially available fertilizers should be used at about a quarter of their recommended strength for three successive waterings. The fourth should be a pure water rinse to flush out any soluble salts that have accumulated. This is referred to as "constant feeding." For many years, good general advice has been to begin fertilizing in the spring when new growth appears using a fertilizer such as 15-30-15 about once a week. This fertilizer helps get the plants started. By mid-May to June, as the plants begin to really grow, move to a high-nitrogen formula such as 30-10-10, which provides an abundance of nitrogen for rapidly growing foliage and compensates for any nitrogen that may be taken up by the bacteria that break down the bark. In late summer or early fall, as the growths are maturing switch to a low-nitrogen, high-phosphorus, and potassium formula such as

All orchids, including *Catasetum* Orchidglade, need to be lightly fertilized. Flush plants occasionally with plain water to avoid the buildup of mineral salts in the pots, which may damage the root tips.

Judicious application of fertilizer has played its part in bringing *Miltonia* Les Chines 'Linda Hara' AM/AOS to flower. For beginners it's best to use a fertilizer specifically developed for orchids and a widely accepted application schedule, as fertilizing with too strong a dosage or too often can cause leaf-tip burn or dieback.

Peter's 10-30-20 Blossom Booster, used to encourage flowering. By October reduce fertilizer applications to once a month or less until spring. This approach suits many growers well. Others have adopted a simpler solution. They use a balanced formula such as 20-20-20 or 17-17-17 at a rate schedule similar to that outlined above, since excess nutrients are not utilized by the plants. Both of these commonly used approaches have served growers well for many years.

It has long been thought that high phosphorus content in fertilizer is responsible for stimulating and increasing blooming in orchids. However, recent research at Michigan State University, published in *Orchids* magazine in June 2003, suggests that the phosphorus needs of orchids are relatively low and that increasing phosphorus levels can increase blooming only if there is a preexisting deficiency. In general, it is the decrease in excess nitrogen that is responsible for more abundant blooming. Since water quality is so important to the way plants utilize nutrients, the researchers at MSU have developed two formulas—one for mineral-rich, or hard, water such as most well water (19-4-23), and a second for relatively pure water such as RO (13-3-15). The MSU researchers' approach does not so much contradict tradition as it clarifies what actually happens in the plants. The results achieved in growth and flowering with the MSU orchid collection have so far been remarkable and compelling. The bottom line is that orchids need supplemental nutrition and that there are many ways to address their needs.

In general it is best to use fertilizers formulated with ammoniac or nitrate sources of nitrogen rather than urea, which does not break down as readily under normal orchid-growing conditions and can be washed out of a pot before it becomes available to the plant. This information is available on the labels of most fertilizers in the form of percentages and can be useful in deciding whether to purchase a particular brand. Giving too much nitrogen throughout the year generally results in a number of problems: Lush green growths that may be too soft and can't support themselves well are more susceptible to disease and either inhibit or prevent flowering.

Regardless of the specific fertilizer or formulation, it is important to consider the other nutrients besides nitrogen, phosphorus, and potassium. Many fertilizers now include all the necessary macronutrients and micronutrients. For those that do not, fertilizers such as Peter's 15-5-15 Cal Mag or micronutrient supplements such as Peter's S.T.E.M. can be used to provide these elements. If you grow just a few plants, try distributing crushed oyster or eggshells on top of the medium or working it into the medium to provide calcium. You can use Epsom salts at the rate of one teaspoon per gallon of water once a month to provide magnesium. Or sprinkle a very small amount of crushed dolomitic limestone on top of the mix to provide both nutrients.

Some growers prefer natural fertilizers such as diluted fish emulsion or composted manure, soaked in water and strained. Both provide the necessary macronutrients as well as trace elements. Disadvantages are a fixed NPK ratio and foul odor.

Fertilizer applied in liquid form while watering tends to be the most controllable and convenient method of feeding. Solid fertilizers such as the time-release types Nutricote and Osmocote provide constant amounts of fertilizer at every watering over a specific period of time, determined by the rate at which the fertilizer breaks down. These are not recommended for general use on all orchids as they can deliver too much fertilizer and burn leaves and roots. They are often a useful supplement to a regular fertilizer program for heavy feeders that grow quickly such as cymbidiums, lycastes, and catasetums.

There are numerous other supplements such as vitamins and silicon that are passionately advocated by some growers. There are constantly new fads in fertilizers and regimens, but beginning orchid growers are probably best served with a fertilizer specifically developed for orchids and a widely accepted application schedule.

Growing Media and Potting

Orchids grow in or on almost anything, which seems antithetical to their reputation as demanding exotics but also accounts for the proliferation of cultivation techniques and growing media. Most commonly orchids are grown in pots, but wooden baskets and mounts are also very popular.

Pots, Baskets, and Mounts

Pots When orchids are grown in pots it is easier to deliver consistent moisture to the roots and to keep the plants upright. Terra-cotta and plastic are the two most widely available materials. Terra-cotta pots are porous and "able to breathe"—that is to say, they allow air exchange. They let moisture evaporate through their walls and dry relatively quickly. These properties make them ideal homes for many orchids, such as cattleyas. Terra-cotta pots are also heavy, an asset in keeping top-heavy plants from toppling over.

By putting any potted plant inside a slightly larger terra-cotta pot (double potting) the porosity of the clay effectively cools the roots of temperature-sensitive plants. If the outer pot is kept damp, the moisture that evaporates from its surface helps to cool the inner pot. The effect can be enhanced by placing a layer of damp sphagnum moss in the space between the inner and outer pots. Double potting is particularly beneficial in hot climates or during the heat of summer for sensitive orchids such as masdevallias and other pleurothallids. Drawbacks of terra-cotta pots are that they are relatively expensive, fragile, and hard to sterilize. It can also be difficult to remove a plant from a terra-cotta pot without having to break the pot and risk injuring the plant.

Lightweight, thin-walled plastic pots are now the vessels most commonly used commercially and probably the best choice for beginners. They are easy to ship, inexpensive, and retain moisture well, and it's usually possible to remove plants from them without injury. They are also relatively easy to clean and sterilize. The two biggest disadvantages are that they topple over easily and become brittle with age.

Choosing which type of pot to use is a matter of accessibility, cost, and the moisture needs of the plant that's moving in. Pleurothallids, for example, need to stay constantly damp and are therefore easier to grow in plastic pots. Both plastic and terra-cotta pots need to have several holes in the bottom or sides to promote drainage. Specialized clay

Clay pots especially made for orchids have side slits to increase drainage and air circulation. Regular pots made of plastic or terra-cotta are equally suitable for orchids, and it's always possible to make extra holes to improve drainage and ventilation as needed.

Orchids with a rambling habit, those requiring impeccable drainage, and those with pendant inflorescences such as *Promenaea* Crawshayana (*P. stapelioides* × *P. xanthina*) are typically grown in baskets. Their open structure allows for good air circulation, which helps to keep the root systems healthy.

orchid pots have additional slots cut into the sides to increase drainage and access to air, but it's not necessary to buy these. Regular pots work just fine, and it's always possible to cut additional holes into plastic as well as terra-cotta pots to improve drainage.

Baskets In the 19th century orchids were most commonly grown in baskets. Though similar in use to pots, baskets tend to be chosen for plants with a rambling habit (*Bulbophyllum*), those requiring impeccable drainage (*Vanda*), and those with pendant inflorescences (*Stanhopea*). They are also commonly used for large specimen plants. Their open structure allows for good air circulation, which helps keep the root systems of large plants from staying too wet and rotting. Baskets range from about 4 inches to 16 inches or more across. They are typically made of ¾-inch wood strips, alternately stacked log-cabin style and secured with wire posts at the joints. This creates openwork containers with generous gaps all around. Plastic net versions are also usually available in smaller sizes, up to 8 inches, occasionally as large as 12 inches.

Mounts Mounted directly onto branches, pieces of cork bark, or tree fern plaques, orchids can grow somewhat naturally. Rambling and climbing types such as many bulbophyllums, miniature dendrobiums, and some oncidiums need to be grown in this way. Many orchids that resent repotting often benefit from being mounted. The roots of a mounted orchid can spread freely, and drainage and exposure to air are perfect. Horizontal plaques or mounts are usually referred to as rafts.

Growing Media

Several factors need to be considered when picking a growing medium: drainage, water retention, resistance to decomposition, and compatibility with the plant, as well as cost, availability, and environmental concerns. Most potting mixes available in the United States and Canada are fir bark–based and also include other materials that combine to create a medium that drains freely yet retains varying degrees of moisture.

One of the problems with organic materials like fir bark is that they decompose over time and eventually retain so much moisture that they may suffocate a plant's roots. This is not a problem when working with inorganic media such as lava rock and pebbles, or man-made materials such as perlite, rock wool, and Turface. They last indefinitely without breaking down and drain well while also holding some moisture. Though some of these media can leach small amounts of soluble materials detrimental or toxic to plants, their greatest liability is that many tend to be very heavy. Rarely used alone as a sole medium in North America, inorganic and man-made materials are often added to potting mixes for specific purposes.

ORGANIC GROWING MEDIA

Bark Byproducts of the lumber industry, pine-, fir-, and sequoia-bark chips are usually available in sizes from ¼ inch to 2 inches, and sold in sifted grades as fine, medium, and large. Bark can be used alone, but it appears most often in mixes that include some or all of a number of other materials such as charcoal, perlite or sponge rock, tree fern fiber, and coconut fiber. Fresh bark repels moisture and needs to be watered quite frequently. As it ages and breaks down, it retains more moisture, so watering must be adjusted to avoid overwatering. Bark alone is fairly neutral and will generally last for a couple of years before it needs to be replaced. If not replaced, the bark breaks down into a dense soillike mass that will smother and eventually kill orchid roots.

Coir and coco chips Coconut husks are processed into either long-stranded fibers, called coir, or into coco chips, which are similar to bark chips. Coir is occasionally used alone or as a lining material for baskets. Coco chips or chunks are most often used as a constituent in mixes. They hold more moisture than bark but also break down more quickly. Fresh chips need to be soaked and rinsed repeatedly in fresh

Orchid-potting materials include, clockwise from top left, fir bark, coir, perlite, New Zealand sphagnum moss, osmunda fiber, tree fern fiber, and, in the center, hardwood charcoal. Most commercial potting mixes are fir bark–based and also contain other materials to create a medium that drains freely.

water to remove high concentrations of salt that can damage roots. Coir, a renewable resource, can hold ten times its weight in water and should be considered as an alternative to sphagnum moss, which faces an all too uncertain future in nature.

Cork The bark of a species of oak native to Spain and Portugal, cork can be harvested every few years without killing the tree. Often used for mounts because of its naturally rough surface and appearance, cork lasts for years and is often a good alternative to tree fern mounts. It is also ground into small nuggets that can be used in potting mixes. Unfortunately, it breaks down fairly quickly and takes on a muddy consistency.

Hardwood charcoal Lasting for a very long time without breaking down, hardwood charcoal is used effectively by itself in some parts of the world, but most often it is added to bark mixes to extend their life span and "sweeten" them by absorbing impurities and soluble salts that can damage roots. It is usually sold in graded sizes similar to bark. Many sources for hardwood charcoal are controversial. Most supplies are a product of large-scale burning of hardwoods from tropical forests to produce fuel for cooking fires.

Osmunda fiber For many decades before the use of bark mixes became widespread, osmunda was the medium of choice for orchid growers. Made from the fibrous root system of certain *Polypodium* and *Osmunda* fern species, it is long-lasting, retains moisture well, and does not require the addition of nutrients. Osmunda is soaked in water to soften it, then packed tightly around the orchid's roots. Collecting osmunda is labor-intensive, and the medium has become increasingly expensive.

Sphagnum moss Harvested from bogs, sphagnum moss is a popular organic medium for orchid culture. It grows all over the world, but the finest quality mosses are found in Chile and New Zealand. Due to overharvesting fueled by the huge demand in the nursery trade, domestic supplies of high-quality sphagnum moss are becoming rare. Be sure to use only sustainably harvested moss, or, whenever possible, use coir as an alternative. Sphagnum moss has a neutral to slightly acidic pH. Highly water-retentive, it drains well and allows air around the roots. If watered frequently, it can easily retain too much moisture, though, and if it is packed tightly around a plant, can lead to root loss. Plants grow well in it, and if humidity is good, plants can go without watering for several days. Sphagnum moss must not be allowed to dry out completely, as it is hydrophobic and must be watered thoroughly several times a few minutes apart to adequately rehydrate it. Sphagnum moss breaks down fairly quickly, especially as a result of fertilizer applications. Plants growing in it need to be repotted within a year. Otherwise the moss will become very acidic and the plants will begin to decline.

Tree fern fiber The fibrous elongated root system or trunk of tree ferns has been used for decades as a medium as well as a mounting material for raising orchids. Its use is controversial, as tree ferns have been increasingly threatened by overharvesting and habitat loss in some parts of the world. Tree fern is still widely used in the tropics as a primary growing medium. Most commercial supplies are now regulated by permits issued in the country of origin, and the material has become more expensive. In North America, tree fern fiber is occasionally used by itself, but most often small amounts of shredded tree fern are added to mixes for plants that are kept wet or need to be disturbed as infrequently as possible. The stiff, dark brown, twiglike strands are long-lasting and provide a skeletonlike structure that helps extend the life of a potting mix.

INORGANIC AND MAN-MADE MATERIALS

Lava rock Used in small chunks, lava rock retains moisture and also drains well. It is used on its own mostly in areas such as Southeast Asia and Hawaii where it rains a lot and the material is abundant. Similar in use to perlite, lava rock is occasionally added to mixes to open them up and extend their life span.

Perlite A heat-expanded volcanic rock, perlite, also called sponge rock, resembles white pumice. Porous, extremely light and airy, and slightly water-retentive, it is often used to lighten and open up orchid mixes and improve drainage. Usually only the larger sizes, ⅛ inch to ½ inch in diameter, are used for growing orchids.

Rock wool Sold in small, chunky feltlike cubes, rock wool is spun from the fibers of melted minerals. It comes in different densities that either retain or repel water. These can be combined to create a medium with specific drainage and water-retention properties. A plant growing in rock wool does not need to be repotted until it outgrows the pot. Algae growth on top of the medium is a common problem.

Turface Small, low-fired clay nuggets, Turface is similar to rock and stone, but as a porous ceramic material it retains a little more moisture.

Repotting in Good Time

Orchids can be repotted at any time of the year if necessary, but it's best to repot as new growth is beginning or just after blooming. Avoid repotting in the heat of summer or as flower spikes are emerging. In general, most potted orchids should be repotted every two years. Some types such as *Phalaenopsis*, *Paphiopedilum*, *Miltoniopsis*, and others with sensitive root systems benefit from being repotted at least every 9 to 12 months. They need to be moved before the growing medium has greatly decomposed, since the medium falls away cleanly from the roots while it's still relatively fresh. These plants can take a long time to recover if their roots are damaged due to poor conditions in their pots. Others such as dendrobiums prefer to be root-bound and do best when they are disturbed as little as possible. They can safely stay in their pots for as long as three years provided that the medium has not completely broken down.

Try not to delay repotting until the growing medium has completely broken down and become dense, muddy, and soillike. By this time the root system will often have been damaged or killed. The foliage may look desiccated and withered, and some of the leaves and growths may have begun to yellow or fall off. To the inexperienced grower the withering leaves may suggest that the plant is too dry. However, an accelerated watering schedule usually worsens the problem. The survival of the plant depends on immediate repotting. While it is best to remove any

Left: In a sympodial orchid, new growths appear laterally in front of the previous growths. The plant has to be repotted when the new growths come right up to the edge of the pot. Right: A monopodial orchid grows continually upward from the top of the plant. It eventually becomes lanky and needs to be topped.

flowers or inflorescences when repotting, it is absolutely necessary in any circumstance in which the plant appears weakened, such as desiccation, disease, or severe mechanical damage. Otherwise the flowers will drain the energy of the plant and set it back or even kill it.

Regardless of the condition of the medium, orchids always need to be repotted when they have outgrown their containers. For a sympodial orchid (in which new growths appear laterally in front of the previous growths), such as a *Cattleya* or an *Oncidium*, it's time to repot when the new growths come right up to or hang over the edge of the pot and new roots grow outside of the pot. The best time for repotting is when blooming has finished and new roots or growths are emerging.

A monopodial orchid (in which there is continuous upward growth from the top of the plant) like a *Phalaenopsis* or *Vanda* eventually becomes unmanageably tall and lanky and needs to be topped. This can be done almost any time of the year.

Repotting a *Phalaenopsis,* this page and opposite: First spread paper over the work surface and pick out a new pot. Remove the plant from its old pot, gently squeezing it to ease out the plant. Live roots are green and whitish. The old medium has not broken down much, a sign that the timing is appropriate.

Repotting Step by Step

You need a pot, an adequate amount of growing medium, disposable plastic gloves, several sheets of newspaper or craft paper, and sterile single-edge razor blades or a knife. Depending on the type and size of the orchid, other materials and tools may be needed such as stiff No. 10 wire, a hammer, pliers or a wire cutter, string or twist ties, and wire or wood stakes appropriate for the size of the plant.

REPOTTING A SYMPODIAL ORCHID

For a sympodial orchid, select a pot that will allow at least two years of new growth in front of the most recent one. You can move the entire plant into a larger pot or divide it by separating the front few growths and potting these separately. The smallest division should have no fewer than four growths including new emerging leads. For more detailed information on dividing, see "Vegetative Propagation," page 62.

Spread a sheet of newspaper over the work surface. Then, wearing gloves or making sure that your hands are clean, gently take the plant you want to repot in one hand (if possible) and use the other to remove the old pot. If a plant grown in a terracotta pot is very root-bound, gently tap the rim of the pot with a hammer or the side of a pair of pliers to loosen it. If the plant is growing in a plastic pot you may have

Carefully remove the old potting medium from the orchid roots. Then cut off any injured, rotting, or dead roots with a disposable single-edge razor blade. Move the plant into its new pot. Gently ease fresh growing medium in between the orchid roots until the pot is filled.

to squeeze the pot in several directions to loosen the plant. Occasionally you may have to break or cut the pot off. Be careful when handling the plant—new growths and roots are easily bruised or broken, and any damage to the plant tissues can provide an easy entrance for disease organisms.

Clean as much of the old medium off the roots as is easily possible without damaging or breaking them. Remove dead roots, which can be recognized as dark brown, soggy, or papery with the old exterior tissue (velamen) easily peeling away. Live roots are typically white to light brown and succulent with glossy green or red tips. Also take the time to remove all old dead sheaths, leaves, and pseudobulbs.

Before setting the plant into its new pot, some people like to place polystyrene packing peanuts or broken pot shards in the bottom with the idea of improving drainage. This is a matter of personal preference and is not absolutely necessary. Place the sympodial orchid with the older growths up against the edge of the pot so that there is room in front for new growths. If the roots are too abundant or too long to fit into the new pot, try curling them around inside or trim them to about four inches in length. A word of wisdom: Do not determine the needed pot size by testing the plant's fit in pots intended for other orchids, or you risk spreading viral diseases. Hold the orchid in position so that its base, or rhizome, will be just at the surface of the

Topping a monopodial orchid, this page and opposite: Spread clean paper over the work surface. Remove hanging wires and plant label from the basket. Using a new single-edge razor blade, cut off the top of the stem. Move the top portion to a new basket and tie it in place with wire to hold the plant upright.

medium once the pot is filled. Pour in a small amount of slightly damp potting mix, working it in among the roots. Gradually add more medium until the pot is filled. Then, using your thumbs, press the medium somewhat tightly down around the plant. The mix should be compressed just enough so that it would be possible to pick up the plant by its foliage without the (plastic) pot falling off. The plant must be very secure in its pot and should not wobble. A wire "rhizome clip" is often used to hold the plant down in its pot and prevent it from falling out. This is especially important for top-heavy plants such as cattleyas. In some cases it will be necessary to tie the growths to a stake to properly support them.

REPOTTING A MONOPODIAL ORCHID

A monopodial orchid such as a *Vanda* usually produces additional roots along the length of its stem as it elongates, and it is usually fine to cut off the top 14 to 24 inches of the stem and move it with its roots into another pot or basket of the same size. Often small lateral shoots will develop on the old plant. Other monopodials like *Phalaenopsis* or pseudomonopodials like paphiopedilums and phragmipediums are cultivated in pots that are just large enough to accommodate their root systems. A plant with a ten-inch leaf span should fit into a pot no larger than four to five inches

If possible, carefully turn the basket upside down to wire the base of the plant to the bottom of the basket. Then turn the basket upright and add growing medium, such as the charcoal shown here. Reattach the hanging wires. Note the repotting date on the plant label and put it back in place.

in diameter. Do not move these types of orchids into a pot that's considerably larger than necessary. All the extra medium holds more water than the plant can use, which will invariably lead to root or rhizome rot.

Unlike sympodial orchids, these plants should be placed in the center of the new pot. Carefully add the medium around the roots and compress, as described above. A rhizome clip is rarely necessary, though a stake may be needed for taller top-heavy plants.

REPOTTING A BASKET-GROWN ORCHID

When you are planting an orchid into a basket rather than a pot, line it with coir, sphagnum moss, or another material that prevents the medium from falling out and allows the roots, growths, and inflorescences to push through. Otherwise proceed as described above for a pot. If the roots of a plant grown in a wooden basket have completely covered the slats, set the entire basket into the next-larger-size basket, adding fresh lining and mix as needed to fill in any voids.

MOUNTING AN ORCHID

A mount material is chosen to allow an orchid to grow and spread naturally over a long period of time without being disturbed. It needs to be able to retain a little

Some orchids grow best when mounted, such as this *Ornithocephalus inflexus*. Hold off on growing orchids on mounts until you've had some success with potted orchids.

moisture and have sufficient texture for roots to attach well. Tree fern and cork bark plaques and the branches of trees that are slow to rot, such as cypress (*Cupressus*) and sassafras (*Sassafras albidum*), are good choices. The mount should be no larger than necessary to accommodate a few years of growth. Start by attaching a sufficient length of stiff wire to the mount near the top. Bend it into a hook and use it to hang the plant up in its new home. Position the bareroot plant firmly with its rhizome against the mount, (taking care not to unnecessarily crush the roots) where it will grow up along or cover the surface. Place a small pad of sphagnum or osmunda over most of the exposed roots to help retain some moisture while the plant gets established. Finally, secure the plant and moss to the mount with wire, monofilament fishing line, or other material such as nylon hosiery strips that lasts long enough for the orchid to grow and attach itself, usually at least a couple of years. Tie it firmly to its support so that it can't move, but be sure that the wire or line does not cut into the rhizome or damage the growths. Overwatering a mounted plant is almost impossible. In fact, quite the opposite is true. Maintaining good humidity is vital, and it may be necessary to water a mounted plant daily. Beginners, especially those without access to a greenhouse, should certainly experiment with growing orchids in pots before trying to cultivate mounted plants.

Once the orchid is in its new home, be it a pot, basket or mount, replace the name tag, adding the repotting date if you like. Place the plant in the light conditions it prefers, but hold off watering for a few days to allow any cuts or broken roots to callus. Water sparingly until new growth resumes, then go back to regular watering.

Maintaining Proper Sanitation

Be sure to use a sterile blade if you are making a division or need to trim off dead or dying plant parts. The easiest way to transmit diseases such as viruses, which are incurable, is to use the same cutting tool on two different plants without sterilizing it in between. When working with gardening shears or a knife, one method of sterilization is to flame the blades with a propane torch before moving to another plant. Unfortunately, though this often damages the tool, the blades need to be heated until they turn red, or any virus fragments that adhere to them may survive and be passed on to the next plant. You can also sterilize your cutting tool in a concentrated bleach or sodium hydroxide solution. Prescrub the tool with a scouring pad and then soak it for at least 20 minutes to make sure that it is sterile. The easiest way to ensure good sanitation when making any cut is to use a new, inexpensive single-edge razor blade for each plant and then discard it. Remember, one plant per blade. Of course, you can collect the blades for reuse until they become too dull by sterilizing them in an oven for two hours at 400°F.

Always work over a fresh sheet of newspaper or craft paper and discard it after each plant. In this way you avoid the chance of transferring the sap from an infected plant to a common surface that may later infect another plant. When you're finished with one plant, replace the gloves with fresh ones or wash your hands thoroughly with a disinfectant soap before going on to the next orchid. Avoid allowing a plant to touch a surface or medium that may come in contact with another plant. Absolutely never reuse potting mix or an unsterilized used pot, even if it appears in good enough condition for another orchid—it may carry disease organisms.

Cleanup should include disposing of the used newspaper, gloves, and blades, any used or contaminated medium, and excess plant materials. Finally, wash your hands thoroughly before moving on to the next project.

Growing Orchids Under Lights

Patti Lee

Simply put, light is life. Plants require light for photosynthesis, to convert light energy and carbon dioxide into sugars and starches. Plants use these carbohydrates for cell building—growing and flowering. When orchids grown indoors fail to flourish and flower, insufficient light is often the cause.

Without the benefit of natural sunlight, supplying proper light indoors can be challenging. Different types of orchids have entirely different light requirements, and how well they do under artificial lights depends on how well these needs are met.

Spectrum is an important aspect of light to be considered when setting up an artificial lighting system. Natural sunlight comprises all colors, with red at one end of the spectrum and blue at the other. Plants need a combination of blue, to promote growth and roots, and red, to encourage flowering and fruiting.

Another aspect of light is intensity. Light intensity is measured in foot-candles or expressed as lumens or lumens-per-watt in gauging light output from a lighting system. Both measurement units are based on the intensity of light emitted from one candle at a distance of one foot. The higher the foot-candle number, the more intense the light, and the higher the lumens-per-watt, the more efficient the light fixture. Most orchids require between 800 and 4,000 foot-candles, depending on the species. For orchids grown under artificial lights, the rule of thumb is the more light the better.

Depending on the conditions in your home, you may have to supplement the available natural light with artificial light to bring orchids such as *Perreiraara* Luke Thai 'Catherine' HCC/AOS to bloom.

Duration is yet another vital consideration. Blind tests using plants of the same size and age grown in otherwise identical conditions have shown that 10 to 16 hours of fluorescent lighting are needed per day, with 14 hours optimum. (The same number of hours applies for other lighting systems.) Other studies suggest that a lack of intensity can be offset and compensated for by longer exposure to less intense light. Extending the duration of light exposure, therefore, may be an answer to medium to low light intensity. It's important to bear in mind, though, that plants require at least four to eight hours of darkness to grow properly. Some orchids also need a period of shorter days to initiate blooming, so be sure to check cultural instructions for specific species. Consistent, even light requires greater attention to other aspects of culture. If orchids are given more light, they will grow and transpire more and require more water and fertilizer.

Light quality is also important. It can be measured using the Color Rendering Index, or CRI, which indicates how close the light emitted by a light source is to the color of natural light, described as CRI 100. Another way of measuring light quality is by its Kelvin rating, which is based on the color emitted by a heated carbon instrument. Carbon heated at low temperatures emits a red-orange light and is designated by a low Kelvin rating. At higher temperatures the light emitted is very blue and has a high Kelvin rating. Kelvin ratings approaching that of daylight, which is 5,000 K, are the goal for an indoor setup.

Systems generating light for orchid growing vary considerably in cost, attractiveness, and installation requirements. There are many indoor light gardens, Wardian cases among them, that are both utilitarian and attractive and unlikely to offend family and friends when they are displayed in the home. Other larger or more complex lighting units may be better suited for setting up in a basement or a room devoted to orchids.

Incandescent Lighting Systems

The simplest and easiest, though least efficient, systems employ incandescent bulbs. These are the familiar screw-based plant lights used in clamp-on fixtures, usually with aluminum reflectors. In the past, many bulbs simulated natural color with blue glass or paint to mask the yellow glow of the incandescent filament. Today, bulbs like the Dayspot by Agrosun are specially calibrated with a coating of phosphors (rare earth elements such as neodymium), which allow the filament to emit a fuller spectrum. Full-spectrum bulbs like these are the most effective incandescent systems. The

Cycnoches herrenhusanum 'Jade Heart' was grown by the author under wide-spectrum fluorescent lights. Longer hours of exposure under artificial lights make up what it is lacking in intensity and spectrum.

lumen measurement of a 150-watt Dayspot is between 1,200 and 1,300. And the light color is close to natural light.

Fitted with decorative shades to make them more aesthetically pleasing, clamp-on lights can be attached to shelf edges or pole lamps and aimed directly at plants. Follow the manufacturer's instructions for recommended distances from the plants. Heat from these bulbs can be a concern, so keep fixtures 24 inches or more from plants, depending on the bulb's wattage. If you put your hand on the orchid's leaves, you can gauge the amount of heat emitted by the bulb on the back of your hand: If it's too hot for you, it's too hot for the plant.

Fluorescent Lighting Systems

Fluorescent systems are more energy efficient and cooler operating than incandescent systems. The tubes are long-lived, lasting from 10,000 to upwards of 33,000 hours. (For comparison, household incandescent bulbs last about 500 hours, and the new incandescent plant bulbs last about 3,000 hours.) Note the date when you are installing or replacing fluorescent lights; manufacturers usually recommend that the tubes be replaced every year, as lumens (light output) decrease in time.

Tubes are available in various lengths, but those between 48 and 96 inches are the most efficient for orchid growing. Wattages for most tubes are length-related:

Usually, the longer the tube, the higher the wattage. For example, a 24-inch tube provides 20 watts (975 lumens), and a 48-inch tube provides 40 watts (2,450 lumens, or about 62 lumens per watt). It's best to choose the longest unit possible for the available space, as there's never too much light for orchids growing indoors.

Fluorescent tubes are generally described as emitting "cool white" (blue-green) or "warm white" (red-orange) light. Neither cool white nor warm white tubes alone supply the full spectrum of light that orchids need to grow or bloom properly, but the problem can be somewhat alleviated by combining the two. However, orchids need to be far enough from the lights to benefit from the blending; otherwise they receive cool white light on one side and warm white on the other. It's also important to remember that the cool white–warm white combination still does not approach full spectrum.

Full-Spectrum Fluorescent Lights

Full-spectrum technology provides a better option for growing orchids indoors. Newer tubes such as Agrosun's fluorescents, Verilux's TruBloom fluorescents, and Westron's Spectrumlites supply a spectrum that's over 90 percent true and 20 percent brighter than other grow tubes. This is achieved by using a combination of rare earth phosphors, including, again, neodymium, which alters the quality of the light emitted to a fuller spectrum.

The spectral balance of these tubes is as close to natural daylight as possible. Their CRI is over 90, and since sunlight has a CRI of 100, colors appear almost natural. These tubes also have little "drop-off," or reduced light intensity, toward the tube ends. In ordinary fluorescent tubes the center emits the most intense light, and the intensity goes down by as much as 40 percent toward the tips. To compensate for the drop-off you can place plants under the tube ends closer to the light.

Integral to fluorescent systems are ballasts, which control voltage and electrical current to the tubes. If possible, select fixtures containing electronic ballasts. They cost more than standard fixtures, but they are cooler, more efficient, and less expensive to operate. They use semiconductor components to increase the frequency of lamp operation, thus raising overall efficacy.

High-Output Tubes

Other options for fluorescents are HO (High Output) and VHO (Very High Output) tubes; these have higher wattages for the standard lengths; for example a 48-

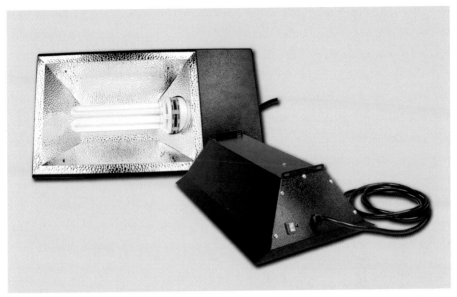

Self-ballasted mogul base compact fluorescent fixture, at left seen from below, at right from the side. The reflective material on the inside of the fixture helps to direct the maximum amount of light to the plants.

inch HO tube provides 60 watts, and a VHO tube provides 110 watts instead of the usual 40 watts for that length. Higher-output tubes are not compatible with standard fluorescent fixtures, requiring their own HO/VHO-compatible ballasts. Again, price may guide selection—the higher-output systems are costlier. Color Rendering Index numbers are not available for these tubes, but Kelvin ratings are. Choose bulbs that are as close to daylight (5,000 K) as possible.

Compact Full-Spectrum Fluorescent Lights

Also relatively new to the market are compact full-spectrum fluorescents, occasionally called power compacts. These may be coiled, U-shaped, or two tubes in tandem. Most of these have built-in ballasts and the familiar screw-in bases that fit into standard incandescent sockets. Until recently, only low wattages were available and the lights were useful for a relatively small growing area, but improvements in the technology are starting to reach the market. For example, Sunlight Supply offers a 95-watt compact fluorescent that has a high output of 60 lumens per watt. It is available at the warmer 2,700 K or the cooler 6,400 K, preferred for orchid growing. Although this particular compact has a mogul base, which requires a larger fixture than standard incandescent bulbs, the reflector hood supplied in the setup has the correct-size socket as well as a special aluminum insert that increases reflectivity. If the unit is put on a light mover (discussed in depth under High-Intensity-Discharge Systems, below), coverage is increased dramatically.

A distinct advantage is that the fixture doesn't have to be mounted very high above the plants. Heat from fluorescents is not as great a problem as it is with incandescent and high-intensity-discharge bulbs. The fixture should be mounted about 24 inches above a shelf or table for smaller plants, higher for taller ones. The distance between the orchids and the lights can be adjusted for different intensities. If the top of a plant is six inches from the center of the fixture, it will receive about 2,000 foot-candles; if it is ten inches away, it will receive 1,500 foot-candles, and if it is a foot away, it will receive approximately 1,000 foot-candles. The Sunlight Supply unit is an excellent choice for anyone favoring a fluorescent system if space is at a premium. The 95-watt, 15-inch compact bulb can replace two 40-watt, four-foot standard-output fluorescent tubes, and it supplies more light as a bonus.

Still another option incorporating fluorescents is PFO Lighting's Start n' Grow hood fixture, an all-purpose, rather complicated combination of HO fluorescent tubes and high-intensity-discharge (HID) bulbs (discussed below). Both fixtures, along with their individual ballasts and a factory-installed cooling fan, are placed in

the same reflector. The fluorescent and HID systems can be controlled independently, which is necessary to run the fixture efficiently, since each system requires that the plants be placed at different heights. Orchids need to be placed rather close to the fluorescent system and farther from the heat of the HID bulb. This arrangement can be useful for growing younger plants under the fluorescents, switching to the HID system when the orchids mature and need more light to flower.

The top shelf of the light cart is fitted with an Agrosun HID lamp. The bottom fixture uses four Verilux fluorescent lamps. Be sure to mount plant lights at an appropriate height to avoid leaf burn.

Arranging Plants Under Fluorescent Lights

When growing orchids under fluorescent lighting, the tops of the plants should be 2 to 12 inches or more away from the tubes, depending on each orchid's light requirements; the closer a plant is to the tube and its center, the stronger the light it receives. For maximum light exposure, raise the plants closer to the bulbs by staging them on inverted flowerpots or suspending them from rods attached to the fixtures.

If you grow just a few plants, fluorescent lighting can be supplied easily with fixtures attached under shelves or in tabletop growing units. However, if you are growing a lot of plants, you may be better served with larger units or prefabricated garden-cart systems. These are available in various sizes and usually have two or more shelves, with two to four standard-length fluorescent tubes over each shelf. For orchids, at least four tubes are needed for maximum light. If you are handy you can suspend fluorescent fixtures from ceiling beams over trays on tables or construct built-in units and stands.

High-Intensity-Discharge Systems

The most energy-efficient artificial light source, high-intensity-discharge (HID) systems provide the most light output per watt and are the most intense of all the lighting choices for indoors. The output of the Agrosun Gold halide bulb, for example, is 40,000 lumens for a 400-watt bulb and 118,500 lumens for a 1,000-watt bulb. For growing orchids indoors, you can choose from three types of bulbs: metal halide, high-pressure sodium, and mercury vapor. (Although they are the most energy-efficient HIDs, low-pressure sodium bulbs are not considered here because their color rendering is unsuitable for orchid growing.)

The basic difference between the HID systems is the type of gas used in the bulbs. As electric current flows through a gas kept under pressure in the bulb, light from different parts of the spectrum is emitted. Metal halides produce light that is blue-green; high-pressure sodium bulbs are more red-yellow, and standard mercury-vapor bulbs emit light in the blue-violet range. Since these provide light from limited color ranges, early setups included both metal halides and high-pressure sodiums, and were switched between the blue-spectrum halides for growth and the red-spectrum sodium bulbs for flowering, imitating the quality of sunlight between spring (blue end of the spectrum) and fall (red end). The setups contained either separate fixtures or a single fixture with both kinds of bulbs, each with its own ballast.

All HID systems require ballasts, which consist of a transformer and a capacitor that energize, or fire up, high-intensity bulbs at the correct voltage and current levels. Low-wattage units can have ballasts built into the fixture; high-wattage units usually have a separate or remote ballast to reduce the weight. The wattage used depends on the number of orchids to be covered, the space allotted for growing, and the limitations of the electrical source. Units are available from 150 to 1,000 watts; 430-watt units are considered maximum for most indoor situations.

Conversion Bulbs

Until recently, metal halide and high-pressure sodium bulbs were not interchangeable and could not be used with the other's ballast. A step forward was the development of conversion bulbs—metal halide bulbs that can be used with sodium ballasts, and vice versa. These are costlier than standard HID bulbs, and their light is not as intense. However, if a halide or sodium fixture is already in place, conversion bulbs are an economical alternative to adding another fixture.

The most recent development is the convertible ballast, which allows the use of either halide or sodium-based bulbs in the same fixture by a mere flick of a switch! It's well worth investing in this system if space or finances allow for only one fixture; the versatility alone is invaluable.

The original spectrum of both the halide and sodium bulbs have also been enhanced and color-corrected to more closely approximate the color of natural light. Thus the Agrosun Gold halide has 40 percent more red than the standard halide bulb, and intensity has been boosted to 100 lumens per watt for a 400-watt bulb. Hortilux and Son Agro bulbs have a 25 percent to 30 percent increase in the blue spectral range and provide 6 percent more light overall (137.5 lumens per watt for a 400-watt bulb) than the standard high-pressure sodium bulb. With these enhanced bulbs, switching between halide and sodium is no longer necessary to achieve maximum results.

Light Movers and Specular Inserts

As energy-efficient as the HID systems are, they can be made even more effective by using light movers—rails or tracks that move the fixture over a growing area at a fixed speed, usually about two feet per minute. This device increases the potential growing area considerably. For example, the coverage of a 400-watt bulb that would otherwise cover an area measuring four by four feet increases to four by ten feet. An added benefit is that plant-growth rates are uniform across the extended span because the light is evenly distributed.

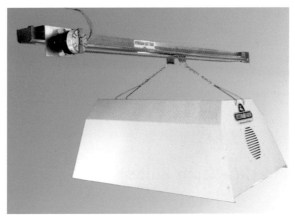

Also available are circular rotating units, such as American Hydroponics' Sun Twist, which has two to five arms that hold lamps of any combination and rotate 180 to 359 degrees, depending on the

Traveling slowly along its track, this light fixture covers a larger area than a stationary unit and also assures even plant growth rates, since its light is evenly distributed across the growing area.

style. A possible drawback is that these units are not particularly attractive. They are best suited to a plant room or basement growing area.

Another way to raise the efficacy of HID light, as well as that of any other system that uses a reflector or hood, is to place an aluminum specular insert inside the fixture. The insert's high reflectivity significantly increases the amount of transmitted light.

Setting Up an HID System

High-intensity-discharge systems are not only energy efficient but, due to their strong light intensity, they also have the widest coverage of all the available systems. Depending on the wattage used, the lights can be placed at a distance between one and seven feet from the plants, which means they can easily accommodate taller orchids and their bloom spikes. An optional feature, almost a necessity, is a tempered-glass lens, a shield that protects the bulbs from splashing water and the plants from the fixture's heat. With the lens in place, you can move orchids that require very bright light closer to the HID fixture for more intense exposure.

A disadvantage of the higher-wattage HIDs is the amount of heat they generate. In

Horizontally mounted Hydrofarm Super Grow Wing fixture with a 400-watt Agrosun high-pressure sodium lamp.

small or confined spaces, this can indeed be problematic, but there are several solutions. Most HID setups offer an optional duct system consisting of an exhaust fan and a hose to vent heat from the fixture. It's also possible to vent the growing space and remove the heat with an exhaust fan installed in a window. In any case, air movement and proper circulation in the growing area is crucial during the warmer months, and in winter, circulating the heated air can also be beneficial.

Mercury-Vapor Bulbs

The final HID option is the enhanced mercury-vapor bulb, such as Westron's Wonderlite. This HID bulb has a chemical compound, phosphorsol, that adds red and far-red to the usual violet-blue range of the mercury burner. This is currently the only wide-spectrum HID bulb that can be used in a standard incandescent socket— a ceramic or porcelain one is recommended—because its ballast is built into the bulb. Though not considered full spectrum, the Wonderlite's spectrum is wide enough to emit a good balance of red and blue, excellent for maintaining orchid growth. However, the lumens-per-watt ratio is lower than that for the others in this group, with an initial output of approximately 6,500 lumens.

Wonderlite bulbs have a built-in reflector, but they can be used in any decorative fixture with a ceramic-based socket, even in a recessed ceiling fixture. They are available as 160-watt bulbs for normal use, as well as 300-watt bulbs for installation in high ceiling fixtures, a boon for orchid growers with larger plants. As with all HID systems, heat generated by the bulb can burn foliage, so keep the plants at a safe distance. Also bear in mind that although increasing the distance also widens the area covered, light intensity is decreased. Check the manufacturer's recommendations.

Wardian Cases

Wardian cases, also called indoor greenhouses, are completely enclosed glass or plastic units that maintain the plants inside in a controllable environment. The units are available in various finishes and sizes—commonly from 24 inches wide by 21 inches deep by 35 inches high to 48 inches wide by 24 inches deep by 42 inches high. Light fixtures are built into the unit's cover or hood along with small fans that circulate the air. The cases usually use fluorescent tubes of the newer biaxial type—high-output double tubes in a tight U-shape, which generate the most intense light available for their size. The hoods are fitted with one to three or more lamp fixtures, depending on the light intensity desired. They have adjustable vent slots to remove the inevitable heat buildup.

Internally, many models are equipped with adjustable shelves for seedlings and racks for mounted or vining orchids. Wardian cases are not intended to accommodate large collections, but they make beautiful display cases for plants in flower or can be used to grow the more difficult species that demand very high humidity—inside a Wardian case the humidity can easily be maintained between 60 percent and 80 percent, even close to 100 percent, if necessary. As it's possible to control conditions inside, the unit may even be used as a recovery area for valuable plants that are ailing.

Some models are fitted with a thermostat and heater to warm the unit if it is kept in a cool area, such as an unheated basement or room. This allows warm-growing orchids to be kept at an appropriate temperature without raising the ambient room temperature.

A possible drawback of the otherwise self-contained unit is a tendency to overheat, especially if it is placed in a warm room. The heat from the tubes and ballasts can add 5 to 15 degrees to the temperature inside the case, a serious problem for cool-growing orchids. This can be remedied by fully opening the exhaust vents in the hood and opening and closing the front doors to dissipate the heat as needed. This is also recommended by the manufacturers to control excessively high humidity. The only practical method of bringing the temperature down, and keeping it low within the unit, is to place it in an air-conditioned room or a cool basement. Currently no mass-produced cases are equipped with self-contained cooling units.

Indoor greenhouses supply good light, and it's easy to maintain adequate humidity levels inside. The only risk is that of overheating, but as long as close tabs are kept on the internal temperature, Wardian cases make growing a small collection of orchids relatively simple.

Orchid Diseases and Pests

David Horak

For decades, the advice for counteracting every insect or disease problem was to use a chemical pesticide. It is foreseeable that at some point in the not too distant future the unlicensed use of pesticides will be restricted in the United States and Canada. Most chemical pesticides require that specific handling and application protocols be followed and specialized safety equipment used. To ignore the manufacturers' guidelines is both dangerous and irresponsible. Even though chemical pesticides are still widely available, you should never use them in the home. There are usually acceptable alternatives.

Despite all the nasty things that can attack your plants, the single most effective solution for most ailments is avoidance. With good cultural practices you can prevent most disease and pest problems or at least keep them in manageable proportions. Both diseases and insects are opportunistic and require certain environmental conditions to thrive. Strong actively growing plants are much more inclined to be resistant and remain healthy than weak or stressed plants. There are dozens of species of insect pests and pathogens that afflict orchids, but for the hobbyist grower, most can be lumped into broad groups requiring similar treatment.

Diseases

Three kinds of diseases affect orchids: fungal, bacterial, and viral. These pathogens most often attack the plants as secondary infections of tissue that has been damaged

When orchids spend the summer outdoors, they will have the occasional insect visitor such as this katydid. Be sure to check your plants for insect and other pest infestations before you move them indoors in fall, and submerge pots in water for an hour to drive out unwanted creatures.

by poor cultural practices or by insect wounds, cuts, scrapes, and other mechanical damage.

FUNGAL DISEASES

Almost always a result of too much moisture and stagnant air, most fungal diseases begin as yellow (chlorotic) spots or areas on the leaves and leaf tips, pseudobulbs, or rhizomes that gradually become brown or black. Leaf-spotting fungi (*Cercospora* species) are relatively benign but unsightly. Affected areas develop dry, dark spots or patches, sometimes sunken, and usually there is a distinct margin between unaffected and damaged tissues. In most cases the damage is only cosmetic and limited to disfiguring spots. However, some fungal diseases such as black rot, caused by *Pythium ultimum* and *Phytophthora cactorum,* are very watery, smelly black infections that can gradually consume an entire leaf, pseudobulb, or lead. These organisms commonly affect *Cattleya*-type orchids. If the affected parts are not quickly removed, the infection can quickly spread and kill an orchid within a few days.

Normally, the best treatment is to remove a diseased plant part, cutting into the green healthy tissue away from the affected area with a sterile blade (new single-edge razor blades are ideal), and apply to the cut powdered cinnamon or cinnamon paste, a remarkably effective natural fungicide. Neosporin ointment may also be used. In the case of fungal rots, this must be done as soon as an infection is discovered and before it reaches the crown or rhizome of the plant. The affected plants should then be kept dry for a few days before normal watering is resumed. Often, watering early in the day so that the plants will be dry by nightfall and increasing the air movement around the plants will prevent fungal problems. The occasional prophylactic use of Physan, a specialized general-purpose disinfectant, can help prevent and treat many problems. Certain plants such as zygopetalums and in particular the popular hybrid *Oncidium* Sharry Baby are notorious for developing spotted leaves.

Other fungi attack and kill the roots of plants. This is a common problem caused by chronic overwatering and decomposed potting medium, which create constantly soggy conditions in the pot. The symptoms are the gradual desiccation of the leaves and lack of vigor. Eventually the lower leaves will yellow and fall off. When this happens, take the plant out of its pot immediately, remove all the dead roots, dust with powdered cinnamon, and then allow the plant to dry for a couple of days in a moderately humid area where it will not become desiccated. Repot it in fresh medium and keep it in a humid environment with only an occasional sprinkling of water until new

Left: Watery spots indicate bacterial rot on the leaves of this *Miltassia*. Cut off affected plant parts with a new single-edge razor blade right away. The earlier you catch an infection the greater the chances for the plant's survival. Right: Fungal disease has affected *Cattleytonia* foliage. Cut off affected parts immediately.

roots begin to grow. Then resume normal watering, watching the plant closely for signs of overwatering. Watering less often and repotting before the medium breaks down can usually prevent the problem.

Seedlings, freshly removed from a flask, are particularly susceptible to damping off—fungal rots that can quickly kill the small plants if they are kept too wet. Certain fungal diseases such as *Fusarium* wilt kill off the tissue in the rhizome of a plant, preventing the transport of water and nutrients, which causes the plant to wither and slowly die. An infection with *Fusarium* appears as a brown or purple discoloration in the rhizome tissue. The only hope for the plant is to cut away the affected rhizome and growth until only clear healthy tissue remains. Sprinkle the cut ends with powdered cinnamon or a simple water and cinnamon paste and leave them to dry for a couple of days. Repot the plant and keep it on the dry side, but in a moderately humid environment for about a week before gradually beginning to water lightly. Regular watering can resume by the second week. This disease can often be prevented by avoiding watering during cool, damp, cloudy weather, when the plants do not dry quickly.

BACTERIAL DISEASES

Usually more insidious, bacterial diseases begin as discolored watery areas or blisters on the leaves, in the new growths, or on crowns of plants such as *Phalaenopsis* and paphiopedilums. The watery spots quickly spread and turn brown or black as the cells collapse. They often give off a distinctive sickly sweet odor. *Erwinia* infections, or bacterial crown rot, which are common on *Paphiopedilum* leaves, usually start near the leaf tips as dark brown watery rot that quickly spreads through the entire leaf and moves down toward the crown of the plant. Bacterial black spot is caused by *Pseudomonas cattleyae* and commonly attacks *Phalaenopsis,* although its botanical name suggests otherwise. Also referred to as crown rot, this disease can quickly spread to the center of the plant and kill the growing point, or meristem.

This *Potinara* has been infected by tobacco mosaic virus. Viral diseases are incurable. Discard affected plants right away to avoid spreading the infection.

The key to contending with a bacterial infection is quick response. Once the infection reaches the rhizome or meristem tissue there is virtually no hope of rescuing the plant. The best response is similar to that with fungal diseases: Remove the affected part of the plant well into the healthy tissue and do not allow the watery fluid to contact any other plant. Treat with cinnamon or Physan as for fungal infections above. If the disease is caught quickly, some *Phalaenopsis* will eventually produce new growths near the base of the main plant. The best recourse for badly infected plants is to destroy them.

VIRAL DISEASES

Viruses are incurable pathogens that are occasionally transmitted by insect vectors but usually passed on by growers using the same blade or shears on several plants without sterilizing in between. There are at least 32 viruses that affect orchids, but the most common are *Cymbidium* mosaic virus (CYMV) synonymous with tobacco mosaic virus, which usually causes chlorotic (yellowish) mottling in new leaves that eventually become patterned sunken brown spots, and *Odontoglossum* ring spot virus (ORSV), which usually appears as chlorotic areas that progress into patterns of black, concentric, sunken ring-shaped lesions. Bean yellow mosaic virus (BYMV) is particularly destructive to pleurothallids and is spread by aphids, which suck out plant juices and transmit the virus as they move from plant to plant. These and other viruses often cause color breaks in the flowers—blotchy or streaky disruptions in the regular pigmentation. Infected plants often gradually decline, and some eventually die. Unfortunately, it is very difficult to diagnose a virus infection based on symptoms alone. Some plants never manifest visible symptoms but can only be diagnosed with serological tests. However, keep your eyes open for any plant that shows patterned chlorotic areas on leaves (especially on new growth) that become black with time; watch out for gradual loss of vigor; and, especially, look for flowers that show symptoms of color breaks.

Plants suspected of a viral infection should be isolated and then tested or destroyed. If a plant is particularly valuable it is tempting to continue cultivating it, but always beware that it can serve as a source for further infections in a collection. The best preventative measure is to treat every plant as if it might be infected. Use blades or shears that are sterilized before use on each plant, or even better, disposable single-edge razor blades.

Pests

Pest infestations are rarely a direct cause of orchid death, but if not quickly discovered, heavy infestations can seriously weaken a plant and lead to secondary fungal or bacterial infections, which *can* be lethal. The wise orchid grower diligently eliminates insect and other pest infestations as quickly as possible.

The most common orchid pests are aphids, mealybugs, scales, spider mites, and thrips, as well as slugs and snails. Aphids, mealybugs, scales, spider mites, and thrips are sucking creatures that consume the juices in the plant cells and in severe infestations can cause leaf loss or deform or destroy inflorescences and flower buds. Aphids, mealybugs, and scales excrete a sweet honeydew prized by ants, which actually "farm" them. The presence of ants often signals an infestation.

Mealybugs on a *Miltonia*. You can avoid most pest and disease problems by providing the right growing conditions.

Aphids

Plump little soft-bodied insects about $\frac{1}{16}$ of an inch in length, aphids are often brown, green, black, cream-, or peach-colored. They form groups of individuals that most often attack new growths, inflorescences, buds, and flowers. They are very mobile and spread easily. Their implication in the transfer of bean yellow mosaic virus makes them particularly worrisome pests.

Mealybugs

A common pest that forms masses of individuals on new growths, leaves, inflorescences, and buds, mealybugs are cottony, soft-bodied, lozenge shaped insects up to about $\frac{1}{8}$ of an inch long. Both juveniles and adults are slow movers. Infestations are easy to treat but can be difficult to eradicate if they get down into the roots. Vigilance is the best defense. Unpot the plant and thoroughly search for the invaders using a cotton swab and rubbing alcohol, rinse off all the old infested medium and repot the plant.

Scales

Either hard or soft-shelled brown bumps up to $\frac{1}{8}$ of an inch in length, scales are most often found on the undersides of leaves and on flower stems. As juveniles, or crawlers, they are mobile and can move from plant to plant. As adults they become fixed in place. Boisduval scales are particularly destructive, especially to cattleyas, and are very difficult to eradicate once they have infested a plant. The males can form huge colonies of white cottony, rod-shaped masses that superficially resemble mealybugs. The females have a typical soft brown helmet shape. Most often they are found on the leaves and pseudobulbs, often hiding under dead bracts.

Spider Mites

Minute arachnids, spider mites are nearly invisible to the naked eye. Usually they aren't discovered until a plant is severely infested. They attack the individual cells in leaves, causing a silvery white appearance with masses of tiny webs on the leaf undersides.

Thrips

Small insects that jump around when disturbed, thrips are usually brown to black and about $\frac{1}{16}$ of an inch long. They attack and destroy leaves and flower buds by sucking juices from plant tissues, leaving a scraped appearance.

Controls

Aphids, mealybugs, scales, spider mites, and thrips can be controlled without pesticides, though they may not be entirely eliminated. The key is persistence. One of the best methods of control is to maintain a clean collection. Remove dead leaves and sheaths

The best way to rid your orchids of slugs is to take advantage of the animals' nocturnal habits and to hunt them down with a flashlight once they have started to emerge after dark.

where insects can hide. Rubbing alcohol applied with a cotton swab also works well for mealybugs and aphids, though less so for scale. Both mealybugs and scales can be squished and rinsed off, though the immature crawlers may be difficult to see. Spider mite infestations can be difficult to treat. Washing each leaf individually with mild soap and water can be effective, which is easiest to do in a small collection.

Insecticidal soaps (which are actually concentrated chemical salts) and especially horticultural oils (such as Sunspray horticultural oil, a highly refined form of mineral oil) applied as sprays have proven very effective against most sucking insects without damaging plants.

Neem oil, derived from the neem tree (*Azadirachta indica*), native to India, is applied as a spray and is an effective and relatively safe natural pesticide. Hot pepper wax is a highly refined wax fortified with capsaicin derived from hot peppers. It is intended to act as a deterrent rather than as a treatment. Occasionally, other remedies are advocated. As with any new product or technique, try it on a plant or two before applying it to your entire collection. For all commercially available controls, follow the manufacturer's instructions.

Slugs and Snails

Potentially very destructive, slugs and brown snails (bush snails) usually appear at night and can consume large sections of flowers and new growths in a few hours. They normally prefer moist areas and hide inside or under the pots during the day. A number of nonchemical remedies exist, such as diatomaceous earth sprinkled on surfaces adjacent to where the pots are set. Its microcrystalline structure abrades and irritates the "foot" of these pests and acts as a deterrent. But the only truly effective nonchemical solution is to take advantage of their nocturnal habits. Wait until a couple of hours after dark and then, using a flashlight, hunt them down after they have emerged to feed.

Propagating Your Orchids

Your orchid collection probably includes plants that have been propagated using several different techniques. Orchids, like many other plants, can be propagated sexually, by seed, or asexually (vegetatively), using plant parts other than seed to produce clones of the parent plant. Traditional vegetative propagation techniques such as division and the removal of offsets are the methods used by most small-scale growers. Propagation by seed took a big step forward in the mid-1920s, when Dr. Lewis Knudson of Cornell University developed a formula for germinating orchid seeds in sterile flasks containing plant nutrients, a carbohydrate source, and agar. The most recent advances in propagation involve tissue culture, or meristemming, a form of high-tech vegetative propagation. These discoveries have enabled orchid growers to produce plants faster, in greater numbers, and more cheaply than ever before.

A note on orchid conservation: Vegetative propagation is a basic and effective means of propagating orchid hybrids. However, the long-term survival of orchid species in the wild, especially those that are rare or declining, is best served by sexual propagation because it promotes genetic variation. Propagate the species in your collection by seed, producing seed capsules via cross-pollination. Share plants and pollen with other orchid growers. To increase the plants' conservation value, keep meticulous notes on the provenance of the plants and the pollen. If you are not inclined to raise orchids by seed yourself, you can promote the cultivation of seed-grown species by purchasing specimens that have been propagated by seed. Flasked seedlings are often available and are an inexpensive alternative to mature plants. For more information on threatened orchids, see Appendix I and II of the Convention on International Trade in Endangered Species of Wild Flora and Fauna, better known as CITES (www.cites.org). To find other conservation-minded growers, contact your local botanic garden or the American Orchid Society (www.aos.org).

Species that are endangered in the wild, such as *Paphiopedilum rothschildianum*, should be propagated by seed to promote genetic diversity.

Vegetative Propagation

Charles Marden Fitch

Using vegetative or asexual methods is the most practical way to propagate your orchids at home. Which technique to use depends on whether the particular orchid has a sympodial or monopodial growth habit (see illustration, page 33). Sympodial orchids such as cattleyas and oncidiums have multiple growing tips. Each new growth arises from the rhizome of a previous growth, and each is capable of bearing an inflorescence. The most popular way to increase sympodial orchids is by dividing the clumps. Monopodial orchids such as *Phalaenopsis* and vandas usually have a single, continuous growing point but occasionally offer a side-shoot or stem plantlet. Some orchids produce vegetative offsets called keikis at the base of mature plants or on thickened stems that store water, called pseudobulbs, and some *Phalaenopsis* produce them on older inflorescences or from dormant stem buds. All of these vegetative growths can be used for propagation.

Dividing Sympodial Orchids

Well-known sympodial orchids such as cattleyas and the many hybrids derived from related genera such as *Brassavola, Laelia,* and *Sophronitis* all grow like a rhizomatous iris: They have a creeping rhizome from which new growths sprout from buds each year. Eventually, the new growths develop pseudobulbs. Each mature growth in orchids with pseudobulbs has at least one active growing point, called a lead. At the base of every live pseudobulb, even those several years old, are dormant buds, called eyes.

Divide sympodial orchids when the new lead growths have sprouted and new roots are just starting to form. Spring into early fall is the best time to divide most orchids because plants in active growth are likely to establish quickly with little shock.

Although you can sometimes divide smaller orchids by pulling or snapping apart the clumps, using a sharp sterile cutting tool is a better method. A sharp knife or pruning tool are good choices. If you have many mature clumps to divide, an electric or battery-powered saw is useful. Cut through the woody rhizome to make divisions of one or more active new growths with two to four recent pseudobulbs attached. The older pseudobulbs usually have a few active roots and will provide reserve moisture as new growths establish. Look for live dormant buds (eyes) at the base of backbulbs (old, leafless pseudobulbs that are still alive) that you might otherwise discard. These backbulbs often will sprout a new growth.

Taking a cutting from a sympodial orchid, clockwise from top left: Spread paper over the work surface. Cut off an actively growing new pseudobulb with a new single-edge razor blade. Move the pseudobulb to a new pot. Fill the pot with growing medium. Make a rhizome clip to hold the orchid in place and replace its tag.

Getting a Head Start

You can sometimes get a head start on sprouting backbulbs by cutting halfway through the rhizome from several months up to one year before you plan to repot or divide the clump. Backbulbs will often sprout their dormant buds once the rhizome is injured by a cut. Making this cut gives the backbulbs a good opportunity to sprout while still partially attached to the active newer growths. To discourage rot and stimulate sprouting, dust the cut with a rooting powder such as Rootone (see "Suppliers," page 111).

Preventing Disease

Sometimes a virus-infected orchid plant will not show any typical symptoms such as leaf spotting or flower color breaks, but it can still spread virus to other orchids in the

sap released at dividing time. To prevent disease transmission, be sure to sterilize cutting tools between each orchid clump you divide. Metal cutting blades are best sterilized in a flame (see page 39). A small alcohol burner is one easy way to keep a flame going near your repotting workstation.

Sprouting Backbulbs

Use coarse New Zealand sphagnum moss (see page 31) soaked in a solution of one teaspoon Superthrive liquid per gallon of water to encourage backbulbs to sprout. Put the backbulbs in a well-drained flat, tray, or pot on top of an inch or two of the moist moss. Keep them in a humid, bright location with nights above 65°F. In a few months most of the live buds will have sprouted. Slight bottom heat helps get dormant buds growing. If you have an area that receives warm air from below, such as a greenhouse bench near the heat or the higher shelves in a light cart, put the backbulbs there.

When new roots emerge it is time to pot the new growths. If you do not pot each sprouted bulb after roots begin to form, be sure to keep the moss moist with dilute fertilizer solution and put the newly active orchids in bright enough light to encourage sturdy growth. The plants can grow quite well in the moss, but it is easier to pot them individually before the roots grow long. To make a full clump with several new leads, pot several sprouted pseudobulbs in a single container.

Stem Cuttings

Stems, actually slender pseudobulbs, of *Dendrobium nobile* and other dendrobiums with buds along the stem can be set on moist sphagnum moss or an alternative medium to encourage the growth of new plantlets. If nighttime temperatures are too high, *Dendrobium nobile* hybrids will produce small plantlets (called keikis) along the stems instead of producing flowers. If you want plantlets rather than flowers, just keep fall to early-winter night temperatures above 60°F. The stem plantlets will live for years attached to the original pseudobulb, but it is easier to grow the plants if you pot the plantlets. Propagation from stem cuttings is the method often used by commercial growers in Asia to quickly produce vegetative propagations of popular cut-flower orchids such as *Dendrobium phalaenopsis* hybrids.

Vegetative propagation is a basic and effective means of propagating orchid hybrids, such as *Ottara Hidden Gold 'Talisman Cove'*, opposite.

Backbulbs, old leafless pseudobulbs that are still alive, can be encouraged to sprout, producing additional orchid plants.

Plantlets on Monopodial Orchids

Monopodial orchids, those that normally have a single growing point and no pseudobulbs, may produce plantlets at the base of mature plants. Once these smaller plants have several live roots, it is safe to cut or twist them off for separate potting. *Angraecum*, *Vanda*, *Asocentrum*, and *Doritis* are examples of monopodial genera that often sprout these base plantlets.

If you want to grow a big clump with multiple flowering stems, just leave the base plantlets in place. The plantlets usually take two to three years before they produce flowers.

Plantlets on *Phalaenopsis* Inflorescences

Phalaenopsis, especially species such as *Phalaenopsis luddemanniana* and its hybrids, naturally produce plantlets on older inflorescences. Within one season the plantlets will have several active roots and can be safely twisted or cut off and potted. If you leave the plantlets on the original inflorescence, they will often produce their own flowers after one to two years.

To be sure that a small plantlet is sturdy before you cut it off the parent plant, you can use this procedure: Put some coarse moist sphagnum moss or an alternative medium in a small plastic pot or on a pad of plastic mesh. Secure the mesh or the pot

Phalaenopsis naturally produce plantlets on older inflorescences. These can be removed from the parent plant and repotted.

with horticultural plastic-coated wire twist ties so that it holds the moss around the plantlet base. Rest the plantlet with its moss packet on the pot edge or support it with a stake to keep the inflorescence from breaking. Once the plantlet has filled the moss with roots, you can safely cut it away from the parent.

Plantlets From Dormant Stem Buds

A hormone paste applied to dormant stem buds, most commonly those of *Phalaenopsis*, sometimes will encourage plantlets to form. One such product is called Keikigrow. A similar hormone paste, Keikiroot, stimulates roots to form on plantlets.

Tissue Culture

Tissue culture or meristem propagation of orchids is a high-tech form of vegetative propagation best done by a trained laboratory professional (see "Micropropagation of Orchids," page 76). Fortunately for hobbyist orchid growers, several orchid propagation labs offer tissue-culture services for retail customers. These laboratories will contract to grow orchids from buds (meristems) of a new growth or culture dormant stem buds from *Phalaenopsis* to obtain stem propagations. A typical contract involves a modest payment for the initial propagation procedure (culture in sterile flasks on nutrient agar), and then a second payment based on the number of plants you desire from the resulting mass of new cells.

Raising Orchids From Seed

Joseph Arditti and Yam Tim Wing

For centuries, orchid seeds and how to germinate them remained a mystery. *Shih Ching* (*The Book of Songs*), published in China 2,500 to 3,000 years ago, and the writings of Theophrastus (370–285 B.C., or about 2,300 years ago) include the earliest known references to orchids, but they do not mention seeds. The first person to describe and draw orchid seeds was the Swiss naturalist Conrad Gesner (1516–65). However his *Opera Botanica*, which contains the illustrations, was not published until between 1751 and 1771, some 200 years after his death. As a result, the first published description (more general and not as detailed as Gesner's) was by Georgius Everhardus Rumphius (1627–1702), a German-born employee of the Dutch East India Company in Ambon, Indonesia, who gained fame as a naturalist and is considered the founder of orchidology in Southeast Asia. His monumental six-volume *Herbarium Amboinense* was published between 1741 and 1750, 40 years after he died. The first description of orchid seedlings was published in 1804 by the British botanist R.A. Salisbury (1761–1829).

Almost 50 years passed before David Moore (1807–79), director of the Glasnevin Botanical Gardens in Ireland, found a way in 1849 to germinate orchid seeds under horticultural conditions. Moore's method led to widespread germination of orchid seeds in British orchid nurseries and eventually to the first horticultural hybrid, *Calanthe* Dominyi, in 1856.

The biological principles that made this type of germination possible remained unknown for many years, since neither the growers nor the scientists of the day were aware of the role played by mycorrhiza, fungi that form symbiotic associations with orchid seeds that enable them to germinate. This is surprising, because orchid mycorrhiza were apparently first noted in 1840, positively recognized by 1846, and their existence was firmly established by 1886.

In 1899 the French botanist Noël Bernard (1874–1911) discovered that penetration by a fungus is required before orchid seeds germinate in nature. Bernard formulated a method for germinating orchid seed using the fungus, but died before he could complete his research. His method, known as symbiotic orchid seed germination, was effective but cumbersome, because it required the culture of two organisms—a fun-

Methods through which seed are germinated on specially designed media have made propagation by seed easier, especially for tropical epiphytes such as *Aerides houlletiana* × *A. flabellata,* opposite.

gus and the seeds. Germination was also erratic, and the fungus often killed some or all of the seedlings.

An asymbiotic method in which the seeds are germinated on a medium called Knudson B was developed by the American plant physiologist Lewis Knudson (1884–1958). It was published first in Spanish in Spain in 1921 and a year later in English in the U.S. Following his original discovery, Knudson continued to work on the subject and in 1946 published his improved and now well known Knudson C (KC) medium.

Today, Knudson's method and other asymbiotic methods are widely used for germinating the seeds of tropical epiphytic orchids. Knudson C is not entirely suitable for the seeds of tropical terrestrial orchids like *Paphiopedilum*, which germinate better on specially formulated media. Seeds of species from temperate climates are more difficult to germinate. They do not germinate well on the KC, *Paphiopedilum,* and other asymbiotic media. The seeds of some of these species can germinate on specially formulated asymbiotic media, whereas others require symbiotic fungi, and some are almost impossible to germinate in vitro. The most commonly used asymbiotic methods, which are suitable for the great majority of cultivated orchids, will be described here. For information on other methods, see the references listed on page 109.

Orchid Seeds

Most orchid seeds measure 0.5 mm to 1.2 mm (0.02–0.05 in.) in length, but they range from 0.05 mm (*Anoectochilus imitans*) to 6 mm (*Epidenrum secundum*). *Dendrobium insigne* (0.9 mm) and *Galeola nudiflora* (0.93 mm) are among the widest orchid seeds. Few orchid seeds have been weighed. Those that have are very light, ranging from 0.3 mg to 0.4 mg (South American *Anguloa*) to 14 mg to 17 mg (Asia-Pacific *Galeola*).

Orchid embryos are also small, ranging from 0.042 mm by 0.058 mm (*Acanthephippium sylhetense*) to 0.19 mm by 0.29 mm (*Dendrobium*). They may consist of as few as ten cells. Embryo volume ranges from 5.85 mm^3 (*Corallorhiza*) to 0.45 mm^3 (*Dactylorhiza*). The volume inside the seed coat can be as large as 81 mm^3 (*Limodorum abortivum*) and as small as 1.14 mm^3 (*Odontoglossum*). The differences between seed coat and embryo volumes can be large, and as a result the proportion of air-filled space inside orchid seeds can be very high (92 percent in *Epipactis palustris*, for example). This enables orchid seeds to float in the air for extended periods and disperse over long distances.

Orchid embryos do contain food reserves in the form of starch and fat droplets, but they lack the metabolic machinery to use them. Consequently, orchid seeds can-

Orchid seeds are tiny and in nature require the penetration of mycorrhizal fungi for germination.

not germinate in nature without becoming associated with a fungus that provides some nutrients and growth factors. The fungus also penetrates orchid roots, where it remains throughout the life of the plant. It is therefore known as mycorrhiza, meaning root fungus.

Germinating Seed

The asymbiotic method of orchid seed germination is relatively simple but requires care and close attention to details. Basically, it involves sowing the seed under aseptic (sterile) conditions on an agar-based medium such as KC in a bottle or flask. (Agar is a gelling agent made from algae; gellan gum, a bacterial product sold as Gelrite or Phytagel, is also used to solidify media.) The popular term for this type of seed germination is flasking. When the seedlings become crowded they must be removed and divided among several flasks that contain KC supplemented with banana homogenate (the edible portion of banana homogenized in a blender) and darkened with activated vegetable charcoal. This process is called transflasking. Once the seedlings become large enough to crowd the second (and sometimes third) flask or bottle, it is time to move them to a "community" pot or flat. This is the stage at which many hobby growers who raise plants from seedlings acquire their plants from commercial laboratories or nursery suppliers (see "Suppliers," page 111).

Seeds can be germinated when they are fully mature after being removed from a ripe fruit as it starts to dehisce, or split open (orchid fruits, often called pods, are actually

At an orchid lab in Thailand, an agar medium containing ripe banana homogenate is prepared for orchid seedlings ready to be transferred to another flask.

capsules). It is also possible to germinate immature seeds (erroneously called ovules) from unripe capsules (erroneously referred to as green pods). Germinating seeds from unripe fruits saves time because it is not necessary to wait until the capsules are fully ripened. A good but not iron-clad rule of thumb—which means that caution is necessary—is to harvest fruits when they are two thirds or three quarters ripe.

PREPARING THE MEDIA

All nutrients of each medium should be added to water (see "Germination Mixtures," on the facing page). Next, heat the mixture and add the agar, stirring to dissolve it before putting the medium into culture vessels (gellan gum should be stirred into medium at room temperature). The vessel should be about 20 percent full of medium. After the gelling agent is added, the culture vessels must be sterilized in an autoclave or a pressure cooker for 20 minutes. Since pressure cookers can vary, a test run is a good idea. If a sterilized medium becomes contaminated after standing for a few days, you will need to start over with a new batch of medium, extending the sterilization time. Water that will be needed in subsequent steps can also be sterilized by autoclaving or pressure cooking.

STERILIZING UNRIPE CAPSULES

Undamaged unripe capsules are not split and have thick walls. This simplifies sterilization because sterilants cannot reach and damage the seeds inside the fruit. To sterilize

Germination Mixtures

No.	Component	AMOUNT Tropical epiphytes (Knudson C)	Paphiopedilum (RE)
	MINERALS		
1	Ammonium nitrate, NH_4NO_3		400 mg
2	Ammonium sulfate, $(NH_4)_2SO_4$	500 mg	150 mg
3	Calcium nitrate, $Ca(NO_3)_2 \cdot 4H_2O$	1 g	150 mg
4	Magnesium nitrate, $Mg(NO_3)_2 \cdot 6H_2O$		100 mg
5	Magnesium sulfate, $MgSO_4 \cdot 7H_2O$	250 mg	
6	Manganese sulfate, $MnSO_4 \cdot 4H_2O$	7.5 mg	
7	Potassium nitrate, KNO_3		400 mg
8	Potassium phosphate, KH_2PO_4	250 mg	300 mg
9	Chelated iron[a]		
	(a) Chelating agent, Na_2EDTA	37.3 mg	37.3 mg
	(b) Iron sulfate, $FeSO_4 \cdot 7H_2O$	27.8 mg	27.8 mg
	SUGAR		
10	Fructose		20 g
11	Sucrose	20 g	
	COMPLEX ADDITIVE		
12	Ripe banana[b]	100–150 g	100 g
	DARKENING AGENT		
13	Vegetable charcoal[c]	2 g	2 g
	SOLVENT		
14	Distilled water[d]	to 1000 ml	to 1000 ml
	SOLIDIFIER		
15	Agar[d]	8–12 g	10–16 g

[a]The original recipe does not include chelated iron, but it is preferable.

[b]Use only in transflasking medium for seedlings, not for seed germination.

[c]Animal charcoal must never be used.

[d]**For seed germination of epiphytic orchids (Knudson C medium):** Add items 2, 3, 5, 6, 8, and 9 to 800 ml of distilled water (item 14) and mix well. Adjust pH to 5.2 to 5.5. (The simplest method for doing that is to measure the pH with indicator paper and if it is too high add a few drops of weak (0.1N) acid, then measure again and add more if needed. If the pH is too low, add a few drops of weak (0.1N) base like sodium or potassium hydroxide or ammonia.) Add sugar (item 11), raise volume to one liter with distilled water (item 14), bring mixture to a gentle boil, pour in the agar (item 15) slowly while stirring and keep stirring until it is dissolved. Then add the charcoal (item 13) and mix well. Distribute into culture vessels, cover, and sterilize. **For seedlings of epiphytic orchids (Knudson C medium):** Add items 2, 3, 5, 6, 8, 9, 11 and 12 to 700 ml of distilled water (item 14) and homogenize. Adjust pH to 5.2 to 5, then raise volume to one liter with distilled water (item 14). Bring mixture to a gentle boil, pour in the agar (item 15) slowly while stirring, and keep stirring until it is dissolved. Add the charcoal (item 13) and mix well. Distribute into culture vessels, cover, and sterilize. **For** *Paphiopedilum* **seeds (RE medium):** Add items 1 to 4, 7, 8, and 9 to 800 ml of distilled water (item 14) and mix well. Adjust pH to 5.0 to 5.4, add sugar (item 10), and raise volume to one liter with distilled water (item 14). Bring mixture to a gentle boil, pour in the agar (item 15) slowly while stirring, and keep stirring until it is dissolved. Add the charcoal (item 13) and mix well. Distribute into culture vessels, cover, and sterilize. **For** *Paphiopedilum* **seedlings (RE medium):** Add items 1 to 4, 7, 8, 9, 10 and 12 to 700 ml of distilled water (item 14) and homogenize. Adjust pH to 5.0 to 5.4, and raise volume to one liter with distilled water (item 14). Bring mixture to a gentle boil, pour in the agar (item 15) slowly while stirring and keep stirring until it is dissolved, addd the charcoal (item 13) and mix well, distribute into culture vessels, cover and sterilize. Additional media for orchid seed germination have been formulated and can be used.

an unripe capsule, scrub it thoroughly (a used toothbrush is appropriate) with running water and a household detergent. Rinse well. Then dip the capsule in 70 percent ethyl alcohol for 30 to 60 seconds. Rinse with sterile (preferably distilled or purified) water. Repeat the alcohol dip and subsequent rinse once or twice. Then split the capsule to remove the seeds. Never use wood or methyl alcohol, which is very toxic; isopropyl or rubbing alcohol is safe.

Household bleach (diluted one part to five parts distilled water) or a saturated calcium hypochlorite solution can be used instead of alcohol, but in this case you must immerse the fruits in the sterilizing solution for 10 to 20 minutes. Such a prolonged soaking in a hypochlorite solution may discolor or damage the outside of the capsule, but this does not matter if the seeds inside remain untouched.

Epidendrum radicans with ripe seed capsules, top, and one open capsule, bottom.

Prepare saturated calcium hypochlorite solution: 1) suspend 7 g of the powder in 100 ml of distilled water; 2) stir vigorously; 3) allow it to stand until a precipitate is formed; 4) repeat steps 2 and 3 three times; and 5) decant the yellowish solution for use. Add 2 to 3 drops of household liquid detergent or baby shampoo to the calcium hypochlorite to facilitate wetting. Because this solution can lose potency, it must be used within 8 to 12 hours. Caution: This solution will bleach clothing and irritate the skin. Use safety glasses and make sure you have adequate ventilation.

No matter which sterilizing solution you use, be sure to rinse the fruits with sterile, distilled water afterward. Note: This sterilization procedure is not suitable for fruits that have split or have cracks that may allow the sterilant to reach the seeds.

STERILIZING MATURE SEEDS

Suspend the seeds in a calcium hypochlorite solution for 20 to 30 minutes, shaking vigorously for 30 seconds every 2 to 3 minutes. Then decant the sterilizing solution and wash the seeds with sterile distilled water several times.

SOWING THE SEEDS

To sow seeds from sterilized unripe capsules, scrape them from inside the fruit, then spread a small amount on the surface of the medium in each flask. Remove mature seeds from the sterile distilled water in which they were washed two or three times, then spread a thin layer on the surface of the medium.

WORKING AREA

All work should be done in a sterile hood.

MAINTAINING THE CULTURES

Keep the flasks that contain seeds at 20°C to 25°C (70°F to 78°F) about 30 cm to 50 cm below two 40-watt cool white or plant-growth fluorescent tubes. If you use cool white fluorescent tubes, two low-wattage incandescent lamps should also be installed on the fixture. The lights can be kept on continuously or for 8 to 12 hours per day.

TRANSFLASKING

Within a few months after germination the flasks will become crowded with small seedlings. Move them to a new culture vessel with medium containing fresh banana homogenate and charcoal. This must also be done under sterile conditions. Use a sterile spatula, a wire loop, or a pair of forceps to handle seedlings. The seedlings are fragile and should be handled with care.

REMOVING SEEDLINGS FROM CULTURE VESSELS

When the seedlings reach a size appropriate for planting (usually two to five leaves and two to five roots) in community pots, remove them from the culture vessels. If the vessels have wide necks, place the bottles in body-temperature water for 30 to 60 minutes to soften the agar. The seedlings can then be pulled out easily with a wire loop or forceps. If the seedlings are too big it may be necessary to break the bottles. The seedlings should be soaked in and washed with lukewarm water until the agar is removed, then rinsed with a good anti-damp agent according to the instructions on the package.

COMMUNITY POTS

Pot the washed seedlings in a well-drained seedling-potting mix in community pots (generally 7 cm to 10 cm or 3 in. to 4 in. diameter, but other sizes can also be used) and grow them in a greenhouse under conditions appropriate for the particular plants.

Micropropagation of Orchids

Joseph Arditti and Yam Tim Wing

According to conventional wisdom, French plant scientist Georges Morel (1916–73) was the first to use shoot tips to propagate orchids. Morel is also credited with being the inventor of the method that today is called tissue culture or micropropagation. Nothing can be further from the truth. The first shoot tips and meristems (not of orchids) were actually cultured in 1945 and 1946 by Ernest A. Ball (1910–97) at North Carolina State University and by Shih Wei Loo (1907–98), then a graduate student at the California Institute of Technology and later at Columbia University, working independently of each other. Morel seems to have used Ball's methods in his work without properly crediting him. In 1948, Arthur W. Dimock at Cornell University in New York used micropropagation of shoot-tip cuttings to free *Dahlia* plants of spotted wilt virus. The fact that the culture of shoot tips can be used to free plants of diseases was called to Morel's attention by two of his colleagues, but he failed to mention their help in his initial publication in English ("Producing Virus-Free Cymbidiums," *American Orchid Society Bulletin* 29 [1960]: 495–97), which was more of an announcement than a scientific paper and basically content-free.

The first orchid was tissue cultured in 1949 by Gavino Rotor (d. late 1990s). Rotor was still a graduate student at Cornell University when he successfully cultured *Phalaenopsis* flower-stalk sections. Hans Thomale (1919–2002), a German nurseryman, was the first to culture an orchid-shoot tip, and he published his work in 1956 and 1957. Morel was well aware of Rotor's and Thomale's work but did not cite their accomplishments until after he became revered in orchid circles.

Contrary to accepted scientific customs and practices, Morel's first report, published in 1960, was devoid of any useful information about techniques and procedures. The first publication on orchid shoot-tip culture that followed accepted scientific citation practices and contained all relevant information was by Donald E. Wimber (1930–97) in 1963. Morel should be credited only with coining the term "protocorm-like body" (a small tuberlike structure similar to the protocorms produced by germinating seeds) and generating publicity for tissue culture propagation, but not with being scientifically innovative in his work on orchid micropropagation.

In 1949 the first orchid was propagated via tissue culture. Also called micropropagation, this technique is now used successfully with many orchid species and hybrids. Left is *Cymbidium* Red Imp 'Red Tower'.

The term "protocorm" was coined in 1890 by Dutch botanist and director of Bogor Botanic Garden Melchior Treub (1851–1910). Those interested in a detailed history of orchid micropropagation should consult the 1996 paper "Orchid Propagation: The Path From Laboratory to Commercialization and an Account of Several Unappreciated Investigators" (Arditti, J. and A.D. Krikorian. *Botanical Journal of the Linnean Society* 122 [1996]: 183–241).

Explants

Since the first success with *Phalaenopsis* flower-stalk segments and shoot tips of a European orchid, other explants (sections of living tissues removed for culture) have been cultured, including shoot tips of additional hybrids and species such as *Dendrobium*; leaf tips, bases, and sections; root tips and sections; pseudobulb buds and sections; flower stalk buds, tips, and sections; floral buds; and cells from various plant parts. Explants can be taken from both mature plants and seedlings. When explants are taken from seedlings, it is not possible to selectively propagate outstanding cultivars because their quality is not yet known. However, seedling explants can rapidly increase the number of plants when very few seedlings are available. Avoid taking explants for micropropagation from plants that have been produced via tissue culture—this can cause undesirable mutations, especially if high levels of growth regulators are used.

Explants can be removed before or after the donor plant has been surface sterilized. When the explants are taken before sterilization of the donor plant, they themselves must be surface sterilized.

Surface Sterilization

The first step in surface sterilization is thorough washing with water and a mild household detergent. This is followed by a rinse with distilled water and treatment with a sterilant. The most commonly used sterilants are calcium hypochlorite (see page 74 for preparation instructions) or sodium hypochlorite (usually household bleach diluted one part to five parts distilled water), both

Orchid tissue clumps are being prepared for placement in flasks with fresh agar medium.

Orchid plantlets are thriving in whiskey bottles that have been redeployed as culture vessels.

with two to three drops of mild household liquid detergent or baby shampoo, (prolonged exposure to very high concentrations of such detergents may damage tissues, but the very short exposure to the level used for washing will not be harmful despite several incorrect statements to the contrary), and 95 or 70 percent ethyl alcohol. Alcohol is usually utilized only as a momentary dip. Either of the hypochlorite solutions may be used for a more prolonged soaking of the donor organs or explants. Sensitivity of tissues to these sterilants may vary, so follow published procedures carefully and take great care when using a new sterilant-tissue combination. After sterilization, tissues must be washed with sterile distilled water.

Culture Vessels

Erlenmeyer flasks, test tubes, a variety of plastic containers, many different bottles, and assorted jars can all be used as culture vessels. If used previously for any purpose, the containers must be washed thoroughly with soap and running water, then rinsed several times with distilled water. It is best to avoid containers that have been used to store biological materials or toxic or corrosive chemicals. Containers must have covers that allow for air exchange and at the same time prevent contaminants from entering. These include nonadsorbent cotton buns or one- or two-hole rubber stoppers with nonadsorbent cotton stuffed in the holes. The cotton buns or stoppers should be covered with aluminum foil. In some laboratories the flasks are covered only with autoclaved aluminum foil.

Culture Media

Only a few basic media are used for orchid micropropagation. Knudson C (KC); Linsmaier and Skoog (LS); Mitra, Prasad and Roychowdhury (MPC); Murashige and Skoog (MS); and Vacin and Went (VC) are the main ones, but each is usually modified to suit a particular species or hybrid. Various supplements are used to modify media, including the following:

- plant hormones including such auxins as indoleacetic acid (IAA), indolebutyric acid (IBA), indolepropionic acid (IPA), naphthaleneacetic acid (NAA), and 2, 4-diclorophenoxyacetic acid (2, 4-D), and cytokinins such as benzyladenine (BA)—also known as benzylaminopurine (BAP)—isopentenyl adenosine (IPA), and zeatin;

- vitamins—mostly niacin, pyridoxine, and thiamine but also biotin, folic acid, and pantothenic acid;

- complex additives such as banana homogenate, casein hydrolysate, coconut water, fish emulsion, peptone, and yeast extract (these are called complex because their composition is complex and not always fully known);

- a darkening agent such as activated vegetable charcoal (which, for reasons not fully understood, makes the plantlets grow better); and

- solidifier such as agar or gellan gum, which is sold under brand names like Phytagel and Gelrite.

As a result, the number of different media used for orchid micropropagation is actually in the hundreds (see "For More Information," page 109, for sources of media formulations). Each medium must be prepared carefully and in accordance with instructions and/or on the basis of experience. All media must be sterilized by autoclaving. Depending on the medium and procedure, some components may have to be sterilized via filter sterilization (passing the solution through a filter which removes contaminants) or dissolved in alcohol before they are added to the mixture.

Phalaenopsis tissue-cultured plants just removed from flasks are being rinsed before potting.

Culture Conditions

Most explants can be cultured at 22°C to 25°C (74°F to 78°F), with 8- to 24-hour periods of light daily provided by a variety of sources. The best sources are described in the chapter on seed germination, page 68. However some explants may have special requirements for photoperiods and light intensity. For these, it is necessary to consult published methods or to experiment.

Preparation and Care of the Explants

After preparing the medium, the next step is to take a plant organ or part into the laboratory and cut away some portions or section it and/or remove parts like bracts to facilitate washing and surface sterilization and to expose potential explants after that. Then the explants or sections are placed into culture.

Depending on the orchid from which it is taken, the explant can produce one or more plantlets (they are not "seedlings"), as is often the case when *Phalaenopsis* flower-stalk sections are cultured. Masses of undifferentiated tissue (callus masses) and protocorm-like bodies can be produced from shoot tips, buds, and a variety of other explants. The protocorm-like bodies produce shoots, leaves, roots, and, finally, plantlets.

Tissue-cultured orchid plantlets have been transferred from a flask to a "community pot."

The callus masses, plantlets in various stages of development, or protocorm-like bodies are transflasked, or cultured on the same or a different medium one or more times in different containers until the plantlets are ready to be moved to pots.

Since 1960, a large number of orchids have been tissue-cultured, and many methods are described in the literature. Anyone interested in micropropagating an orchid should first try to find an existing method (see "For More Information," page 109). If such a method is not available, it may be necessary to develop a new procedure.

Hybridizing Orchids

Andy Easton

Some purists question the validity of orchid breeding, postulating that any interference with natural species is to be deplored. For me, hybridizing is a singular opportunity to put together what nature cannot, or may not; if the process is ordered, thoughtful, and sustained, then hybridizers can create something that in essence is a living work of art and a reasonably enduring memorial to their efforts.

Developing the Skills

What does it take to become an orchid hybridizer? A Ph.D. in plant genetics is certainly not a prerequisite. What all accomplished hybridizers seem to have in common is the power of observation and a memory for breeding characteristics, both dominant and recessive, of the genera they are working with. It takes time to hone these skills. I remember my first crossing, no First Class Certificate from the American Orchid Society (FCC/AOS) to be sure, but a pretty plant, and the thrill of watching the first seedling's buds swell and open—now, that's a buzz that should be illegal.

What characterizes most brilliant orchid hybridizers is the ability to see beyond the generation right in front of them. The great English orchid breeder, H.G. Alexander, for example, was able to predict that his famous *Paphiopedilum* Hellas 'Westonbirt' FCC/RHS would be the forerunner of a fall-tones dynasty when the plant was first awarded. It took another 20 or more years, possibly because he retired from the orchid business shortly after, but eventually he was proved right, when *Paphiopedilum*

By making informed choices, hybridizers develop beautiful new orchids such as *Paphiopedilum* Julius 'Maria Teresa' CCM/AOS, a cross between *Paphiopedilum lowii* and *Paphiopedilum rothschildianum*.

Hellas became renowned as a parent of bronzes, yellows, greens, and even pinks with awarded offspring in every country where orchids are judged.

Breeding Goals

Not all hybrids are created equal, though. In my experience, orchid hybridizing tends to split into two main avenues: hybridizing for awards and hybridizing for commercial purposes, which in turn splits into cut-flower and pot-plant types. I personally try to work against the split wherever possible. First of all, the judging process with its strict rules and standards should not be considered the only forum for recognizing beauty. An otherwise award-quality flower with an excessively large lip or a rather open shape will never win an award, even though it may be the most wonderful color. It is quite acceptable to say, "I think this flower is beautiful," and to grow and enjoy it for its beauty. We should not let orchid-judging criteria impede our ability to appreciate the innate beauty of a flower.

There are other orchid characteristics that are prized by both commercial growers and hobbyists alike that are not considered in the judging process. In all my hybridizing efforts I set a goal: the best of the fastest. If a plant has not flowered within 36 months of deflasking, I add it to the compost pile. Speed of growth is vitally important for commercial growers, and it's certainly an important issue for many serious hobbyists also. But unfortunately, there's no way we can accurately know the age of a plant presented for award consideration. We may well be looking at a beautiful front-runner of a generation of hybrids, but we could also be oohing and aahing over the slow-growing runt.

Another important characteristic to consider is how long the flowers last. Within the broad range of *Phalaenopsis* with which I come into contact daily, some flowers will

barely last three weeks while others are still perky after three months—a very desirable trait, I like to think. But it seems that some breeders whose eyes are set firmly on superior flower colors that are resistant to fading are blind to how short-lived their latest creations may be.

Paphiopedilum Ogallala 'Berwyn' AM/AOS, a hybrid of Paphiopedilum Hellas and P. Inca.

Oncidium Sharry Baby 'Sweet Fragrance' AM/AOS (*Oncidium* Jamie Sutton × *O.* Honolulu). Sharry Baby continues to be a very popular *Oncidium* hybrid more than 30 years after it was developed.

What You See Is Not What You Get

If hybridizing is such a complicated, time-consuming business, why don't we simply cross high-quality awarded plants to create a series of surefire hits in one generation? Unfortunately, combining the genes of two superior hybrids seldom results in an even greater plant. A much better strategy, one often used by astute hybridizers, is to look at the two orchids behind the plant that was awarded a First Class Certificate. By examining the parents, breeders can make assumptions about dominant and recessive traits for future crosses with the knowledge that these plants can produce superior progeny.

Forgive me if I use the example of a rather old *Paphiopedilum* to illustrate my point. When I was a young orchid grower in the Pacific Northwest, Beall Orchid Company on Vashon Island, Washington, was our local orchid nursery. The irrepressible Gary Baker, a rare grower who combined university training in genetics with an infectious "what if" approach to orchid breeding, bred most of their orchids. Gary died far too young, but not before he had bred *Oncidium* Sharry Baby, among many other wonderful hybrids. He was not the only visionary in the area, though. Almost all the Beall *Paphiopedilum* hybrids at that time were actually created by Bert Wright, a Boeing engineer. One evening in the mid-1970s, Gary phoned to tell me about a plant called *Paphiopedilum* Honda Gold 'Tyrol' HCC/AOS. Beall sold surplus Bert Wright divisions on commission, and Gary said, "You must buy this plant if you buy no other." It was $65 a division, as I recall, no huge risk, so I bought it. "Just breed with it, don't look at the flower," Gary advised. Well, I did look at the flower, and my first thought was that the judges who'd given it an award must have been a team of losers—to me it looked like a $6 pot plant. But I nevertheless used it as a pollen (male) and pod (female) parent. The next spring, the full spectrum of the *Paphiopedilum* Honda Gold progeny was on view. A cross with an equally mediocre *Paphiopedilum* Wallur had spawned a host of award-quality yellows and greens. I picked the best in my opinion and took it to the Royal Horticultural Society in London on a business trip. The plant, *Paphiopedilum* Vashon Sundance 'Sun Lake', received an AM/RHS plus the George Moore Medal for the best *Paphiopedilum* shown to the RHS that year. In looking back now on nearly 15 crosses with this *Paphiopedilum* Honda Gold, I have yet to see one dud, and in every cross we have been able to select at least several award-quality offspring.

Plant Pirating and Mutations

Advances in meristemming that began with genera like *Cymbidium* and *Cattleya* and moved to more difficult types like *Phalaenopsis* and the *Odontoglossum* Alliance have changed the perspective on what makes a good hybrid. Fifty years ago, hybridizers strove for uniformity of seedling offspring. Parents were prized for their ability to give rise to a high percentage of usable seedlings (usually for cut flowers). Now, accolades are often bestowed on a cross from which only one outstanding plant came out of the seedling population. The buyers are largely spared the heartbreaking spectacle of its 250 or so rubbishy offspring. They purchase a meristem selection that's ready to bloom. To be fair, we shouldn't feel too sorry for the breeder with his culled seedlings. In these orchid boom times, even the also-rans will find homes as blooming pot plants.

However, a serious disincentive to a career hybridizer is the current practice of releasing meristem selections without patent protection and the ongoing pirating of new releases by other companies. It's bad enough that commercial plant pirates take someone else's hybrid and reclone it from nonmother plant tissue. Even worse is that the meristems are sometimes recloned from immature plants even before their flowers have proven them to be reasonable copies of the original. In many hybrids the mutation levels from tissue culture can be quite high in cloning, and I still hear the

Cymbidium Tiger Tail 'Talisman Cove', left, and *Cymbidium* Goldrun 'Cooksbridge' AM/AOS, right, are two hybrids derived from *Cymbidium insigne,* a species that has proved to be a useful starting point for orchid breeders, who are always on the lookout for new and beautiful flower colors and patterns.

words of my old genetics professor ringing in my ears: "Ninety-nine percent of all mutations in plants are deleterious." When I see advertisements offering obviously pirated plants I always wish that I could superimpose on them "Buyer Beware."

In the Netherlands, where growth rates are precisely measured, a leading pot-plant producer told me recently that he compared the performance of thousands of young plants derived from original mother tissue in a reputable lab with that of thousands of plants purporting to be the same variety but from pirate laboratories created with nonoriginal tissue and sloppy cloning techniques. Even six months out of flask the premium plants had an edge, and when they bloomed 18 months later, there was no comparison with respect to the number of spikes, plant size, and overall flower display between the originals and the cheap knockoffs. It was an easy decision for him to pay a little more for quality starting stock.

Pioneer Hybridizers

We have been blessed as plant breeders with the legacy of orchid scientists like Don Wimber and Gustav Mehlquist. Hybrids between distantly related species that are commonly infertile can now be treated with colchicine, which doubles their chromosome numbers and restores full fertility. However, we are far from having all the answers.

Hybridizers often look to the parents of award-winning plants like this *Odontoglossum* Nancy Crees HCC/AOS when picking orchids for hybridizing, as those plants have already demonstrated that they can produce noteworthy offspring.

Some crosses are winners from the day they are pollinated, and others have surprising and serendipitous results. As in every aspect of life, there is always an element of luck, but the best orchid breeders help make their luck too. Many great and experienced hybridizers like Leo Holguin and Ernest Hetherington, Frank Fordyce, and Keith Andrew are in the twilight of their careers, and too few of the present-day breeders have had the opportunity to soak up their knowledge. It would be a shame if newer hybridizers wasted precious years by making mistakes through lack of exposure to accumulated hybridizing wisdom.

Time is the hybridizer's worst enemy—we tend to measure our lifetime in the number of generations still possible for us to see. Only the octogenarian orchidist H.P. Norton seems completely immune to this scourge and is probably planning his *Phalaenopsis* breeding program through 2025, at least! Even with advances in culture, the generation time in most genera is too long to attract many scientific plant breeders. It is not by chance that the most rapid recent hybridizing advances have occurred in *Phalaenopsis,* which has about the shortest generation time of any major orchid genus.

The Future of Hybridizing

Will orchid hybridizing become so high-tech that we are all put out of business by genetic engineering? I think not. I hope for a productive partnership between the orchid breeders and genetic engineers in the future. Could they engineer rounder, fuller shaped flowers? So far only in computer manipulations. Could orchidist Keith Andrew's dream of a blue *Cymbidium* hybrid be engineered into reality? Perhaps, but with so many characteristics important to orchid enthusiasts, especially multigenically inherited ones like shape and conformation, the good old toothpick-wielding breeder is still indispensable. Nevertheless, if it someday enables me to offer *Cymbidium* or *Cattleya* plants with engineered virus resistance as part of the package, I'm all for genetic engineering.

It would be a pity if in the future all we could buy was cloned orchids, for we currently enjoy something that is almost unique to our hobby. With orchid seedlings we still have the opportunity to buy something of unproven potential and share in the excitement of its first bloom. All orchids are champions until they flower for the first time, and even when they bloom some remain so. Longtime orchid growers may be blasé about much of what they experience so regularly in orchid cultivation, but bringing a seedling to bloom is still one of the greatest joys.

It may well be an orchid with 15 or more generations in its lineage, which can be traced back in an unbroken bloodline to those days when orchid growing was the prerogative of the very rich. Times have changed, but you will have something that is a link to a forgotten age and hopefully a window to an even more colorful and floriferous orchid future.

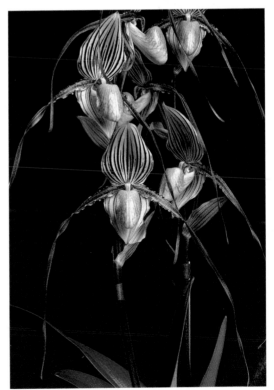

Paphiopedilum **Saint Swithin 'Marie Terese'** **is a hybrid of** *Paphiopedilum rothschildianum* **and** *P. philippinense.*

How to Pollinate a Flower

After selecting the plants to cross, the key to hybridization is pollinating a flower. One plant will serve as the pollen donor, and the other will be pollinated. Sometimes the choice of which plant to use as the pollen plant and which to use as the pollen receptor, or "pod plant," is clear—for example, when one plant is rather delicate and the other is sturdy enough to support the growing fruit. But typically the choice is largely a matter of aesthetics. The hybrid will usually exhibit more genetic influence from the pod plant than the pollen plant.

If the plants do not bloom at the same time, pollinia, or waxy pollen masses, can be stored in glassine or paper envelopes for a year or so. How long the pollen remains viable varies by species, and pollinia stored in paper envelopes will not last as long as those stored in glassine. Be sure to label the envelope, noting the name of the pollen plant and the date the pollinia were removed.

Whether you are removing pollen or pollinating, choose newly opened flowers. Wait a day or two until the flowers mature. When pollinating orchids that produce flower spikes, it is best to use a lower flower on the spike to make it easier for the plant to support the maturing fruit. It is not a good idea to pollinate too many flowers on the same spike.

To remove the pollinia from the pollen-donor plant, cut off the outer flower segments—sepals, petals, and lip—to expose and allow access to the column, the single reproductive structure formed by the fusion of the male stamens and female style. Do this carefully so as not to destroy the flower; a sterile razor blade is an appropriate tool.

Most orchids have a single fertile anther (the flower structure where pollen is produced), located at the tip of the column. Pollinia are under or behind the anther cap, the little dome structure at the top of the column in most orchids. Using a toothpick or sharpened stick, carefully make contact with the viscidium, the sticky tab that holds pollinia together and adheres to the pollinator when contact is made. This typically causes the anther cap to pop off. The viscidium often adheres readily to the toothpick.

When you are ready to pollinate, remove the sepals, petals, and lip of the receiving flower. In this case there is no need to pop off the anther cap. Instead, look for the rostellum, the flap of tissue that separates the pollinia from the stigma, the female part of the flower that receives the pollen. The stigma typically is located in a cavity or depression behind the rostellum. Using a toothpick, push the pollinia up inside the cavity to make contact with the stigma. If they do not adhere immediately, gently scrape the pollinia onto the stigma, being careful to avoid damaging the reproductive parts.

Next, make a paper or plastic label that notes the name of the pollen parent and the date of pollination, and attach it just below the ovary of the flower, or to the flower spike. If the label is paper, be careful not to damage it when watering.

Observe the development of the ovary to determine when it is time to harvest the seed capsule. Within a day or two after pollination, the flower will begin to collapse. Any remaining flower segments will start to wilt, and in a week or two the ovary will begin to swell. The wilted flower parts will dry up and fall off.

If pollination has been successful, the ovary will continue to swell and will remain green over the weeks and months as the fruit matures. If pollination has not been successful, the ovary may begin to swell but will soon yellow, and the flower will fall off.

Seeds can be germinated when they are fully mature. When the fruit, or seed capsule, stops swelling and starts to change color, tie a plastic bag around it to catch the seeds when it splits open. To save time, it is also possible to germinate seeds from a capsule that is two thirds or three quarters ripe, a process called green-pod culture. The green fruit should be removed from the plant when the swelling slows down, certainly by the time the fruit turns yellow and is ready to split open. The amount of time it takes a plant to produce a green pod varies by orchid type, but the average is two to three months. See "Raising Orchids From Seed," page 68, for information on how to germinate orchid seeds.

To successfully pollinate an orchid, you must be able to recognize the flower parts. The orchid illustrated here is a *Cattleya*.

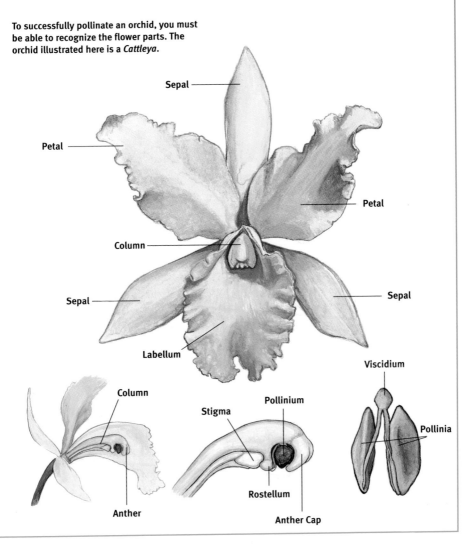

Growing an Orchid Collection

Dennis Dayan

In the spring of 1970, I saw and purchased three *Cattleya* orchids with large lavender flowers. This was the beginning of my addiction to orchids, which has blossomed into a collection of close to a thousand plants including many different species and wonderful hybrids.

Those first three orchids taught me a hard lesson. They all had plant viruses, which are not curable and are highly communicable, and the plants eventually had to be thrown in the garbage. Today, most reputable nurseries will replace any plant sold with a virus, and they are also far more likely to recognize problems and regularly check their plants for signs of disease or pest infestation. Anyone growing orchids has to realize that good sanitary conditions are vital, otherwise a virus or other disease organism present in one plant may be spread through the entire collection. (See also "Cultivating Orchids: Maintaining Proper Sanitation," page 39, and "Orchid Diseases and Pests," page 52.)

In general, for every new orchid coming into my greenhouse, I donate one to an orchid society auction or raffle. I like to keep my collection current and I regularly exchange beautiful plants acquired years ago for current breeding successes and newer hybrids. (See also "Hybridizing Orchids," page 82.)

I initially turned to orchids because I wanted flowers that would bloom in win-

The author won a First Class Certificate from the American Orchid Society for his *Lycaste* Absolutely Stunning 'Sandra Dayan' FCC/AOS.

Lycaste Sunray 'Fortune Dushey' HCC/AOS is one of the many lycastes that lighten up the darkest and coldest months of the year with their exuberant flower display.

ter, and orchids fit my desires perfectly. Starting with cattleyas and cymbidiums, my collection quickly branched out in many directions. My taste in orchids continues to change as I gain new knowledge during orchid society meetings and at orchid shows. I purchase new orchids based on plant habit and how desirable I find the flower, as well as how well the plant will thrive in the growing conditions in my greenhouse.

Arranging the Greenhouse

Living on the New Jersey shore, I am fortunate that temperature swings and violent weather are not as pronounced as in some other areas in North America. I built my first greenhouse in the spring of 1970 from a kit. Made out of wood and glass, it blew apart in a blizzard eight years later. I learned from the experience and now have a greenhouse made of aluminum covered with Lexan, a double-layer polycarbonate. In addition to a propane heater to fend off winter cold and five fans to provide constant air movement, an important accessory in my greenhouse is an evaporative cooler. Mounted in the greenhouse wall, this device pulls in air through a wet pad, which cools the air before it is blown into the greenhouse. In the summer when it's sunny as well as warm outside, an Aluminet shade cloth (woven of aluminum fiber) and three large trees provide much-needed relief from the sun's rays and help keep temperatures bearable, although the thermometer may still go up to 90°F with the cooler running.

Over the years, I've modified the growing conditions in my greenhouse to accommodate my changing tastes. Today my greenhouse is filled with intermediate- to cool-growing orchids. In winter, I try to maintain low temperatures of about 50°F at night, and in summer, I try to keep the temperature under 82°F during the day. I also take advantage of the microclimates in my greenhouse, growing plants that like it warmer and need more light near the heater or higher up, and moving others to cooler spots, such as near the vents (which do leak) and close to the floor or under the benches.

Adventures of a *Lycaste* Lover

I favor lycastes, miltonias, and pleurothallids, but I also have dendrobiums, cattleyas, cymbidiums, oncidiums, *Phalaenopsis*, and other genera. I feel that the genus *Lycaste* has some of the most beautiful flowers in the orchid world. Some of the species in the genus can be grown on a windowsill, and all of them can be accommodated in a greenhouse. There are two popular sections to the genus *Lycaste*: sect. Macrophyllae, generally evergreen, and sect. Deciduosae, the deciduous species, which are usually easier to grow. The flowers are yellow and gold to green and yellow. My favorite in this group is *Lycaste microbulbon* from Colombia, which can have six or more large yellow flowers on each new growth. As with most orchids in this group, they have two sharp spines on top of the pseudobulbs, which you may notice painfully during repotting (it could be worse, though—in the wild, pit vipers tend to nest in these plants). Other lycastes in this section that I enjoy are *L. campbellii*, *L. brevispatha*, and *L. tricolor*. These and the similar *Lycaste macrophylla* need cooler temperatures. I also grow *Lycaste cruenta*, *L. aromatica*, *L. consobrina*, and *L. lasioglossa*, which thrive in warmer temperatures. Some of the warmer-growing plants are hanging high in the greenhouse; others are set near the heater. The cooler-growing lycastes are farther away from the heaters.

A Year in the Life of the Lycastes

This year, for the first time, I moved all of my lycastes outside, hanging them under a pergola at the end of May. There they receive very bright light and suffer only a small amount of leaf burn. The plants appear to benefit greatly from the day and night temperature differential as well as the brighter light. I can fertilize more to support the

Miltonia **Les Chenes 'Linda Hara' AM/AOS displaying its wonderful flowers in the author's collection of around 1,000 tropical orchids.**

plants' accelerated growing pattern in the brighter light and water more often thanks to the constant breezes. Over the summer the plants developed many new growths from the old bulbs, and I can expect substantially more blooms in winter and spring.

At the end of September I moved all my plants into the greenhouse after carefully checking for signs of insect infestation. Healthy plants, and especially those that are hanging, usually don't attract insects, but I'd rather be safe than sorry. As the leaves of *Lycaste* can become quite large, I hang the pots over the aisles and above the edges of the benches at varying heights. The smaller lycastes and those with shorter leaves move to a bench facing south in the greenhouse. They receive a breeze 24 hours a day from the five fans and the evaporative cooler.

In the fall after the new bulbs have formed, the leaves start to yellow and look ratty. They may be cut off or just allowed to fall off. The important point is not to water the plants after the leaves have fallen off. Deciduous lycastes must have a dry rest period in order to flower. Watering resumes when the plants begin to sprout inflorescences.

In the winter, the deciduous lycastes receive almost full sun—the shade cloth comes off the greenhouse in mid-September. The air is much cooler, similar to the conditions in the plants' natural environment, cloud forests high in the mountains. When the plants put up inflorescences in late winter or early spring, I begin to water sparingly and increase watering as the new growths start to show. When the flowers have finished blooming, I repot the orchids in the smallest pots I can fit them into and fertilize liberally. Except for seedlings or newly acquired plants with few roots, I use a bark potting mix; for seedlings and new plants that need to get established, I use New Zealand sphagnum moss in small clay or mesh pots.

My all-time favorite is the Macrophyllae group, which includes *Lycaste skinneri*, in my opinion the most magnificent flower in the genus. The triangular conformation of the three large sepals with the smaller petals elegantly surrounding the lip and column can present a breathtaking picture. One flower, rarely two, on each of the 10 or 20 inflorescences presented on each front growth make a fabulous display. The broad green leaves on these lycastes can frame the flowers as if they were staged.

Lycaste skinneri varies in color from pure white, concolor pink to bicolor, all of which are most desirable. I understand that there is also a yellow form of the species, but have never seen it. *Lycaste skinneri* has large, long-lasting flowers, which I've seen described as satiny, crystalline, waxy, pearly lustrous, glossy, glowing, and polished.

There are more than 365 registered hybrids made with *Lycaste skinneri*, many of them highly desirable. *Lycaste* Shoalhaven is perhaps the best known and most popular. I grow over 30 hybrids in my greenhouse and treasure each one of them. To date I have received five AOS flower awards for *Lycaste skinneri* and *L. skinneri* hybrids. The most exciting of these—and which earned the highest AOS award I have ever received—is *Lycaste* Absolutely Stunning. The cultivar 'Sandra Dayan' received an FCC/AOS, a First Class Certificate from the American Orchid Society, in February 2002 as well as the Huntington award for the best FCC, granted in 2002.

Lycaste skinneri, its hybrids, and the other lycastes in the Macrophyllae group are watered throughout the year and fertilized up through the beginning of November. In December and January, I cut back on the watering for almost all my orchids and give no fertilizer. During this time I can also skip watering entirely for a week or more, which means it's the perfect time for me to go on vacation. By the end of December blooms begin to appear, and they continue into early summer; some of the species will even bloom during the summer months.

Growing *Miltoniopsis*

Along with the lycastes, I have a collection of *Miltoniopsis*. These large flat floriferous orchids put on a great show, bloom from early spring through late summer, and come in every color and combination of colors imaginable. They are all potted in a bark mix in clay or plastic pots. I try to keep them as cool as possible in the summer and repot them every year, after flowering, in as small a pot as they fit into. Keeping them tight in their pots is extremely important, as they can then be watered and fertilized well without risking root rot. I divide them when they become too large for a six-inch pot or when the clump separates naturally when taken out of the pot. When they

Miltonia spectabilis var. *moreliana* 'Linda Dayan' won an AOS Award of Merit for its flower display in one year and a Certificate of Cultural Merit the following year.

start to flower, I move them into the house where it is dryer and consistently around 68°F to 70°F. The flowers expand as they open, and the plants stay in flower for more than eight weeks without any spotting. In contrast to many other orchids, *Miltoniopsis* flowers are not good cut flowers, so it's best to enjoy them on the plants.

I have some of the older *Miltoniopsis* hybrids and species, which I continue to enjoy as well as about 20 new seedlings. I continually buy seedlings from proven parents, and I also make my own. The first blooms on the most recent seedlings have been large, colorful, and very encouraging. I am looking forward to the mature plants and anticipate some wonderful results. I grow seedlings in clay pots and in sphagnum moss until they reach flowering size. At that time, I move them into a bark mix and cultivate them in clay or plastic pots.

Along with the *Miltoniopsis*, which are native to Colombia, I have one very special *Miltonia*, a Brazilian species, *Miltonia spectabilis* var. *moreliana*. My cultivar 'Linda Dayan' was awarded an AM/AOS, an Award of Merit from the AOS. Before I divided the plant it also received a CCM/AOS, a Certificate of Cultural Merit. It had 21 large, dark flowers on 19 inflorescences for the AM awarded in 1995 and 33 intensely colored flowers for the CCM awarded in 1996. With a large collection, it is almost certain that there will always be an orchid in flower. Orchid growers like to joke, however, that the plants seem to know when an orchid show is coming up, and they either bloom too early or too late.

Growing Pleurothallids

I also grow many of the species included in the Pleurothallid Alliance, which thrive in the same atmosphere and growing conditions as my other orchids, but they stay in the greenhouse all year, since it is easier to watch them carefully in the greenhouse. Mostly mounted on tree fern or cork, which many of them have completely covered over the years, these plants are suspended on racks against the back wall of the greenhouse and along the edges of the greenhouse benches. With some exceptions, I grow these orchids in bright shade and water liberally every sunny day except in the winter, when I can skip a week or two.

Masdevallias and draculas grow well in my greenhouse. The draculas are in open clay baskets or mesh pots. I have been growing them in New Zealand sphagnum moss but have been experimenting with Groden mix (rock wool) with sponge rock (large chunks of perlite) added to open it up. I've also mounted some of the more vigorous varieties. The draculas receive direct sun during the winter and bright shade in the summer with a lot of water. They rarely dry out and flower well several times a year.

The masdevallias had been growing in sphagnum moss until I moved them to a bark mix in clay pots, and they seem to be doing much better now. Since the bark

Bifrenaria harrisoniae fma. *alba* 'Marcella Dayan' HCC/AOS is a standout in the author's collection.

In December, the author removes the spent flowers and any new buds from *Dendrobium cuthbertsonii* 'Pink Passion' CCM/AOS and repots the plant, which will send out new growths and buds as the days lengthen in January and February.

mix holds far less water than the sphagnum moss, I can water them more often, which they enjoy. The smaller masdevallias are mounted on tree fern as well as pieces of wood and are thriving and flowering well. I recently put some of the larger masdevallias in tree fern rounds and am waiting for them to become established. I do grow *Masdevallia floribunda*, which needs warmer conditions, on a higher shelf in the greenhouse that receives bright light all year round. I grow *Masdevallia coccinea* and *M. veitchiana* on a shelf close to the floor where they get some sun in the winter but only very little direct sunlight in the summer. I cultivate small *Lepanthes* on tree fern slabs and larger ones in tree fern rounds, which have become covered in moss. These get bright shade all year round. The *Lepanthes* range from the tiny *L. tsubotae* to the comparatively large *L. medusa*. I also have some *Restrepia* species such as *R. antennifera, R. sanguinea*, and *R. cuprea*. These are all growing well and thriving in sphagnum moss, rock wool, and tree fern pots. *Zootrophion dayanum, Z. hypodiscus,* and *Z. oblongifolium* are also all growing in sphagnum moss and have filled their small pots to overflowing. These sit in more sun all year round, and the leaves are tinged in purple. They flower profusely.

Growing Dendrobiums

There is one more beautiful group of orchids, which almost everyone grows—dendrobiums. I cultivate a few of the beautiful New Guinea dendrobiums, which have a reputation of being very difficult—they seem to die without any reason once in a while—such as *Dendrobium cuthbertsonii* as well as *D. cynocentrum*. *Dendrobium cynocentrum* is growing very well mounted on tree fern, and I expect to mount my *D. cuthbertsonii* at the end of this year. The way to grow *Dendrobium cuthbertsonii* was explained to me by an excellent grower: Remove all the flowers and buds in December (or the plant will continue to bloom until it blooms itself to death) and repot the plant. As the days lengthen in January and February, the plant will send out new growths and soon after, new buds.

I also enjoy *Dendrobium mohlianum*. It grows in a basket with tree fern, is watered daily, and receives bright shade, outside, all summer. In the autumn, after the leaves fall, it gets direct sun most of the day in the greenhouse, and it continues to grow in cool conditions. This *Dendrobium* puts out buds on every leafless cane and is a picture of orange flowers in the early spring. I grow *Dendrobium* Kuniko, *D. victoria-reginae*, *D. lawsii*, *D. subclausum*, and *D. obtsisepalum* the same way. I am convinced that the combination of cool temperatures and bright sunlight results in more flowers as well as darker and more vivid colors. Another unusual New Guinea *Dendrobium* that's worth collecting but difficult to grow is *D. violaceum*. Flowers range from dark pink to pale lavender with an orange column. The plant stands out in any collection.

Personal Approach

Every collection of orchids reflects the tastes and preferences of its grower. I'm fond of all my orchids. Each one has a personality, and I check on every one of them as often as possible. I have killed many orchids learning how to grow them, but eventually I was able to do reasonably well with each genus. I have been told that good growers "listen" to their plants. A plant will let you know if it needs something. It's up to the person growing it to interpret the signs. I must admit that I have never been able to grow *Telipogon* or *Disa*. I do not think they like me and, for now, I admit defeat.

Showing Orchids

H. Phillips Jesup

To cover American Orchid Society (AOS) judging in less than a book is a challenge akin to growing species of the nearly uncultivatable genus *Telipogon* in captivity. *The Handbook of Judging and Exhibition*, the judge's bible, consists of 96 pages, but I'll try to squeeze the highlights into these few.

Humans tend to tinker with nature to make it conform to our vision of the ideal—or the bizarre. Sometimes the result is grotesque, as with Pekingese and shar-pei dogs and bubble-eyed goldfish; at other times it's beautiful, as with long-haired dachshunds, silver-spangled Hamburg chickens, and most highly developed lines of orchid breeding (personal prejudice displayed above).

Humans are also competitive creatures. Inevitably, judging systems are developed as formal methods of comparison against an evolved standard. Awards recognize achievement by the breeder of degrees of perfection or testify to acquisition skills by the purchaser. They can be useful in identifying potential parents for future breeding. The AOS awards system is particularly helpful to hobbyists because the listing of a flower award as part of the clonal name of an awarded cultivar (such as *Blc.* Norman's Bay 'Low' FCC/AOS) that is offered for sale as a mericlone or division clearly denotes superiority. And to be grossly materialistic, an awarded plant has greater monetary (and trading) value.

Vanda Rasri Gold 'Orchidgrove' AM/AOS. The letters indicate that the plant has won an Award of Merit, which recognizes flower quality. Outstanding orchids are awarded by the American Orchid Society at monthly judgings held in regional centers around the United States and Canada.

Phalaenopsis **Sogo Musadin 'Aida' AM/AOS won an Award of Merit for its flower quality. Attend a judging to find out if one of your orchids may be award-worthy in the eyes of AOS judges.**

Types of Awards

Showing an orchid is first of all a matter of taking it to a regional judging center on the right day and time. Orchid judging takes place at judging centers in each of 22 judging regions and in supplemental centers scattered throughout the United States and Canada. Judgment on plants or cut flowers submitted to the centers takes place monthly at the same place and time. The dates are staggered among relatively nearby judging centers to give broad coverage. Every month *Orchids,* the magazine of the AOS, devotes a page to dates and locations for each center. In addition, there are a great many orchid shows that are judged by AOS judges. If you have plants in the show, in your own exhibit, or as a contribution to an orchid society exhibit, they will automatically be screened for AOS awards. Some of the larger shows also invite orchid hobbyists to enter a single specimen or a few plants in individual plant classes. If the trip to the judging center is a problem for you or a friend, often a judge who lives close enough will be willing to take your plant to judging for you if you deliver it to (and later pick it up from) the judge's house.

At this point, a clarification is in order: AOS judges participate in two entirely different types of judging. Regular monthly judgings are noncompetitive: Every orchid is judged against a standard of perfection for its particular type. At shows, these dour-looking judgmental types serve double duty: First they "ribbon judge" all plants entered by exhibitors in competition for show awards, giving firsts, seconds, and thirds in each class with the classic blue, red, and white ribbons. Plants are entered in competition in compatible classes, such as "standard cymbidiums," "miniature species and hybrids," and "novelty *Phalaenopsis*." The awards are not recorded except in the show records. At shows judges also grant ribbon awards to competitive exhibits staged by individuals, local orchid societies, or commercial orchid firms, as well as various trophies for best in class for both exhibits and different types of orchids as called for by the individual schow schedule, such as "best exhibit 100 square feet" and "best *Cattleya.*" At the same time, regular AOS noncompetitive judging takes place at the show in the same manner as at monthly judgings. Generally, all plants in the show are eligible to be nominated by the judges for this type of judging unless a plant is clearly marked "not for AOS judging." As with all noncompetitive AOS awards, these are recorded and published in the *Awards Quarterly,* another publication of the AOS, with descriptions and often photographs under the name of the exhibitor. The judges at a show also score exhibits against a standard of perfection for the coveted

Major AOS Awards

FCC/AOS	First Class Certificate	Flower quality scoring 90 to 100 points
AM/AOS	Award of Merit	Flower quality scoring 80 to 89 points
HCC/AOS	Highly Commended Certificate	Flower quality scoring 75 to 79 points
CCE/AOS	Certificate of Cultural Excellence	Cultural perfection scoring 90 to 100 points
CCM/AOS	Certificate of Cultural Merit	Cultural perfection scoring 80 to 89 points
CHM/AOS	Certificate of Horticultural Merit	Granted to a species or natural hybrid for beauty scoring 80 to 100 points
CBR/AOS	Certificate of Botanical Recognition	Granted to a species for characteristics of rarity, unusual interest, and educational value, awarded by a two thirds majority of the judging team without scoring
AQ/AOS	Award of Quality	Granted to a flowering seedling population showing substantial improvement over the type; a minimum of 12 clones exhibited; granted unanimously without scoring *
AD/AOS	Award of Distinction	Granted to a cross which is a desirable new direction in breeding; one or more clones exhibited; granted unanimously without scoring *
JC/AOS	Judges' Commendation	Granted for a distinctive characteristic worthy of recognition, unanimously without scoring *
		* awarded to the exibitor and the hybridizer

AOS Show Trophy, but in this case there is an element of competition, because it goes to the best in the show (although none is given if the judges feel that no exhibit measures up). To garner the Show Trophy, an exhibit must score 80 to 89 points on a scale of 100 for general arrangement, quality of flowers, variety, and labeling. Should an exhibit score 90 or more points, it would receive the rarely awarded Gold Certificate.

A "Good" Orchid

As you become more familiar with the wide, wide world of orchids, you begin to form ideas of what constitutes a "good" orchid, both in flower quality and in cultural perfection, in the eyes of a judge. (See "How Orchids Are Judged," opposite.) Seeing slide shows at local orchid society meetings, observing plants on society show tables, visiting friends' collections, reading, making pilgrimages to commercial growers, and especially going to orchid shows sharpens one's critical eye and broadens perspectives. If your local orchid society has a judge or two among its members, take the plants you think might be candidates to a meeting for the display table and ask for a frank appraisal.

Of course, the only real way to find out if your plant has a shot at an AOS award is to summon your courage and trundle it in to judging. The worst that can happen is that it is not awarded, but even that can be an educational experience, for you should be able to learn from the judges why it was not awarded. You have lost nothing except perhaps the time taken in getting to the center, and you are left with an orchid that *you* think is terrific (or you wouldn't have brought it in). The fact that the judges felt it was not up to the very particular standard for an award should not deter you from your appreciation of its characteristics that appeal to you. Most orchids are not of award caliber, and yet most orchids are beautiful, fascinating, interesting, graceful, or any combination of these qualities.

AOS Judges

AOS judges number in the several hundreds, and there are many additional orchid experts who are in training to join the druid ranks. They are in some ways ordinary people, except that they have been perhaps more seriously smitten by the lure of the Orchidaceae than even most other aficionados. They have the audacity to cast judgment on the quality of an orchid by authority of their formal appointment as judges by the American Orchid Society.

First and foremost, people interested in becoming judges have to demonstrate an intense and steadfast long-term enthusiasm for orchids. This could be said of many

How Orchids Are Judged

The American Orchid Society bestows ten different awards for outstanding orchids. Probably most familiar to hobby growers are the three prestigious flower awards, the First Class Certificate (FCC), Award of Merit (AM), and Highly Commended Certificate (HCC). Judges use a point system to give their awards, but overall, judging is largely a subjective process. The flowers are scrutinized in terms of color, shape, and how they are displayed on their inflorescences. Standards of beauty vary among the many types of orchids, but in general, petals of award-quality flowers are rather flat and do not curl at the edges. Petals and sepals are on the same plane, with none curving forward or folding back. Their general shape tends toward round. Each flower is bilaterally symmetrical: If you draw a vertical line through the flower's center, the two halves are mirror images of each other, and the lip is perfectly bisected. Bright flower colors appear crisp, intense, and saturated. Subtle colors are distinct and clear, not murky. Judges also assess the flowers for flaws: Mechanical damage, water spots, torn petals or sepals or imperfections along their edges, scraped color, and signs of fading in older flowers are all detrimental to an orchid's score.

Beyond the flowers, the judges consider the overall state of the plant before giving an award. For example, faced with an orchid that doesn't appear to be in good condition, the judges may choose not to award it, even though the flowers seem worthy of an FCC, AM, or HCC. By the same token, when they find a plant in prime condition with an outstanding floral display, they may decide to go beyond the flower awards and give the prestigious and rarely awarded Certificate of Cultural Excellence (CCE) or the more commonly awarded Certificate of Cultural Merit (CCM), both coveted by growers.

Each orchid award is recorded and published in the AOS publication *Awards Quarterly*. Documented with slides, the written account is the official record used as reference when a specimen of the same species or hybrid comes up for judging.

Attend orchid judgings to familiarize yourself with the system. See a cross section of the best plants, learn what makes a good orchid in the eyes of AOS judges, and then assess your favorite orchids at home.

It may be pretty, but this *Ascocenda* Princess Mikasa 'Sapphire' would not qualify for an AOS award. In an award-quality specimen, the edges of the petals would be flatter, and the individual flowers would be presented more evenly on the inflorescence.

At orchid shows, ribbon awards are granted to individual plants and competitive exhibits such as this display, which was awarded at the Deep Cut Orchid Society Show.

AOS members, perhaps most. However, orchids must play a major part in the lives of judges, because judgeship is a very long-term, often lifetime, commitment. It's sacrificial, too, because much of what might otherwise be leisure time is spent at monthly judging meetings, judging orchid shows, business and training sessions, and so forth. This cuts into time with one's family, repairing the screen door, and even repotting one's orchids! There is also some cost, such as for travel; judges serve without recompense or reimbursement.

There are other important qualifications, some of which are pretty obvious: The ability to discern and compare and to make independent judgments; high standards of personal integrity; a good fund of knowledge and the desire to expand it; the ability to work with others; and of course, a good interest in all facets of orchidology. Anyone interested in joining the ranks needs to seriously consider the long-term consequences. A candidate for judgeship must complete at least six years of training—first as a student, then as a probationary judge—before becoming eligible for election to full accreditation. Not all who enter the system as students come out the other end as full-fledged judges, for various reasons. Along the route are papers to present, discussions to lead, award slides to critique, and many opportunities to display the depths or shallows of one's knowledge. The wrong answer to the question "Why do you wish to become a judge?" is "I want to learn about orchids." One should know a good deal about orchids before applying for a judgeship; the focus of training and observing after becoming a student judge is in learning how to judge orchids. This is not to say that one should know all about orchids before applying, for no one can know all—we are continually learning.

For More Information

BOOKS

American Orchid Society Handbook on Judging and Exhibition
Eleventh edition
American Orchid Society, 2002

Asymbiotic Technique of Orchid Seed Germination
A.J. Hicks
Orchid Seed Bank Project, 1999

Botanica's Orchids: Over 1,200 Species
Botanica (Editor)
Laurel Glen, 2002

Home Orchid Growing
Rebecca Tyson Northen
Simon & Schuster, 1990

The Illustrated Encyclopedia of Orchids
Alec Pridgeon (Editor)
Timber Press, 1992

Micropropagation of Orchids
Joseph Arditti and Robert Ernst
Wiley-Interscience, 1993

Orchid Basics: A Step-by-Step Guide to Growing and General Care
Isobel la Croix
Sterling Publishing Co., 2000

Orchid Pests and Diseases
James Watson (Series Editor)
American Orchid Society, 2002

Orchids: A Care Manual
Brian and Sara Rittershausen
Laurel Glen, reprinted 2003

Orchids Simplified: An Indoor Gardening Guide
Henry Jaworski
Houghton Mifflin Co., 1997

Taylor's Guide to Orchids
Judy White
Houghton Mifflin Co., 1996

Terrestrial Orchids: From Seed to Mycrotrophic Plant
H.N. Rasmussen
Cambridge University Press, 1995

PERIODICALS

Awards Quarterly
16700 AOS Lane
Delray Beach, FL 33446-4351
561-404-2000
www.aos.org

Orchid Digest
1151 Oxford Road
San Marino, CA 91108
www.orchiddigest.com

The Orchid Review
RHS Subscription Service
P.O. Box 3
Ashford, Kent TN25 6PR, England
www.rhs.org.uk/thegarden/pubs
_journals_orchid.asp
(Orchid journal of the Royal
Horticultural Society)

Orchids Australia
Treasurer, Australian Orchid Council
P.O. Box 145
Findon, SA 5023, Australia
www.orchidsaustralia.com

Orchids
16700 AOS Lane
Delray Beach, FL 33446-4351
561-404-2000
www.aos.org
(Free with AOS membership)

ORCHID SOCIETIES

American Orchid Society
16700 AOS Lane
Delray Beach, FL 33446-4351
561-404-2000
www.aos.org

Canadian Orchid Congress
www.canadianorchidcongress.ca/
index.html

WEB SITES

GardenWeb Orchid Forum
http://forums.gardenweb.com/forums/
orchids/
(Forum for orchid enthusiasts)

Internet Orchid Photo Encyclopedia
www.orchidspecies.com
(Photo encyclopedia of orchids)

Orchid Mall
www.orchidmall.com
(Links to informational and commercial sources about orchids, including
orchid societies around the world)

OrchidSafari
www.geocities.com/~marylois
(Chat site for orchid enthusiasts)

OrchidWire
www.orchidwire.com/about.html
(Source directory)

Sources

GROWING SUPPLIES

Calwest Tropical Supply
11614 Sterling Avenue
Riverside, CA 9250
800-301-9009
www.orchid-supplies.com

Kelley's Korner Orchid Supplies
P.O. Box 6
Kittery, ME 03904-0006
207-439-0922
www.kkorchid.com

Plant Hormones Canada
Dr. James D. Brasch
Box 354, McMaster University
Hamilton, ON, Canada L8S 1C0
www.orchidmall.com/hormones/
index.htm
(Keikigrow and other plant regulators)

Tropical Plant Products
Tropical Plant Products
P.O. Box 547754
Orlando, FL 32854-7754
407-293-2451
www.ken@tropicalplantproducts.com

OFE International
12100 S.W. 129 Court
Miami, FL 33186
305-253-7080
www.ofe-intl.com

U.S. Orchid Supplies
1111 Rancho Conejo Boulevard, #506
Newbury Park, CA 91320
888-492-2647
www.usorchidsupplies.com

INDOOR LIGHTING

Garden Indoors
208 Route 13
Bristol, PA 19007
800-227-4567
www.hydrofarm.com
(Hydrofarm products)

Sunlight Supply
5408 N.E. 88th Street, #A-101
Vancouver, WA 98665
888-478-6544
www.sunlightsupply.com

Orchidarium
16708 Third Street
Riverton, MN 56455
218-546-7700
www.orchidarium.com

Westron Lighting Corporation
3590-C Oceanside Road
Oceanside, NY 11572
800-221-4289
www.westronlighting.com

Verilux
9 Viaduct Road
Stamford, CT 0690
800-786-6850
www.healthylight.com

NURSERIES

A&P Orchids
110 Peters Road
Swansea, MA 02777
508-675-1717
www.aandporchids.com

Exotic Orchids of Maui
3141 Ua Noe Place
Haiku, HI 96708
808-575-2255
www.mauiorchids.com

Haiku Maui Orchids
2612 Pololei Place
Haiku, HI 96708
808-573-1130
www.haikumauiorchids.com

Krull-Smith
2815 W. Ponkan Road
Apopka, FL 32712
407-886-4134
www.krullsmith.com

Norman's Orchids
11039 Monte Vista Avenue
Montclair, CA 9176
888-467-2443
www.orchids.com

Tropiflora
3530 Tallevast Road
Sarasota, FL 34243
800-613-7520
www.tropiflora.com

PROPAGATION SUPPLIERS AND SERVICES

K.M. Chow
300 Alumni Drive, #262
Lexington, KY 40503
www.geocities.com/kmartchow/
kmc_orchid_prop.htm
(seed flasking and *Phalaenopsis* stem
propagation)

Monsoon Flora
P.O. Box 6851
Santa Barbara, CA 9316
805-683-7630
www.monsoonflora.com
(tissue culture and seed flasking)

Orchidland
All China Orchids Corp. Lab
7171 Bark Lane, #1
San Jose, CA 95129
408-725-8129
www.orchidland.com
(tissue culture and seed flasking)

WARDIAN CASES

English Creek Gardens
P.O. Box 516
Williamsburg, OH 45176
800-610-8610
www.englishcreekgardens.com

H. Potter
P.O. Box 6144
Lincoln, NE 6850
402-486-1455
www.hpotter.com

Contributors

Special thanks to the American Orchid Society for allowing Brooklyn Botanic Garden to adapt H. Phillips Jesup's article on showing orchids for this handbook. It was originally published under the title "What Is Orchid Judging?" in the June 1990 *AOS Bulletin*.

Joseph Arditti, professor of biology emeritus at the University of California, Irvine, is a longtime orchid scientist and author of many books and articles on orchid biology and propagation. In 1977 he founded the book series *Orchid Biology: Reviews and Perspectives,* which produced its eighth volume in 2002.

Dennis Dayan is an award-winning orchid grower as well as a certified judge with the Northeast judging center of the American Orchid Society. He has grown orchids since 1970, when he built a wood and glass greenhouse for his cattleyas and cymbidiums. He concentrates primarily on intermediate- to cool-environment orchids, and his collection has grown to include phaphiopedilums, pleurothallids, *Oncidium* Alliance, lycastes, *Vanda* Alliance, and *Phalaenopsis.*

Andy Easton, former director of education and orchid operations for the American Orchid Society, has been growing orchids professionally since 1972. He is currently vice president of life sciences at Kerry's Bromeliad Nursery, in Homestead, Florida, which is one of the largest orchid and bromeliad pot-plant operations in the world. Easton is a keen hobbyist grower of cymbidiums, paphiopedilums, and cattleyas.

Charles Marden Fitch is an internationally known horticulturist and media specialist. He is the author of many books, including *All About Orchids, The Complete Book of Houseplants, Orchid Photography,* and *The Rodale Book of Garden Photography.* His photos have appeared in TV and video productions, magazines, newspapers, package designs, advertisements, and books such as *Ultimate Orchid, The World Wildlife Fund Book of Orchids,* and several encyclopedias.

David Horak has been growing orchids for more than 25 years. He is the curator of Orchids and the Robert W. Wilson Aquatic House at Brooklyn Botanic Garden. He is the current president of the Greater New York Orchid Society and the chairman of the New York International Orchid Show.

H. Phillips Jesup, a banker by vocation and now retired, has been growing orchids since 1952 and is a general horticulturist and naturalist as well. He is active in several orchid societies and is a judge and a former trustee for the American Orchid Society.

Patti Lee has had a lifelong interest in horticulture and floral design. She lectures and writes about various horticultural topics, including growing plants indoors. She helped found the Manhattan Orchid Society in New York City and has created award-winning designs for the Manhattan Orchid Society, the Greater New York Orchid Society, and Carmela Orchids of Hawaii at the New York International Orchid Show.

Yam Tim Wing, who collaborated with Joseph Arditti on "Raising Orchids From Seed" and "Micropropagation of Orchids," is a senior research officer at the Singapore Botanic Gardens, where he specializes in orchid breeding and conservation.

Illustrations

Paul Harwood

Photos

Charles Marden Fitch all photos, except where noted

Sunlight Supply page 45

Hydrofarm page 49

Index

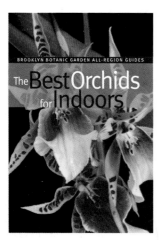

More Information on Orchids for Indoors

The companion to *The Gardener's Guide to Growing Orchids*, *The Best Orchids for Indoors* is a valuable introduction to these exquisite flowers and how they grow. Its beautifully photographed encyclopedia includes culture information and tips from experts about tropical orchids ideal for growing in the home.

Ordering Books From Brooklyn Botanic Garden

World renowned for pioneering gardening information, Brooklyn Botanic Garden's award-winning guides provide practical advice for gardeners in every region of North America.

Join Brooklyn Botanic Garden as an annual Subscriber Member and receive three gardening handbooks, delivered directly to you, each year. Other benefits include free admission to many public gardens across the country, plus three issues of *Plants & Gardens News, Members News,* and our guide to courses and public programs.

For additional information on Brooklyn Botanic Garden, including other membership packages, call 718-623-7210 or visit our web site at www.bbg.org. To order other fine titles published by BBG, call 718-623-7286 or shop in our online store at www.bbg.org/gardengiftshop.